MORRIS MINOR SERIES MM

Ray Newell

CONTENTS

Foulis

Haynes

ISBN 0 85429 412 0

A FOULIS Motoring Book

First published 1984

© **Haynes Publishing Group**

Published by:
Haynes Publishing Group
Sparkford, Yeovil,
Somerset BA22 7JJ

Distributed in USA by:
Haynes Publications Inc.
861 Lawrence Drive, Newbury
Park, California 91320, USA

Editor: Mansur Darlington
Dust jacket design: Rowland Smith
Page Layout: Graham Thompson
Dust jacket colour picture: In the foreground is a 1950 'lowlight' M.M. Tourer, and behind a later 4 door Saloon.
Endpaper picture: An early 'lowlight' model at the BARC Members Meeting at Goodwood in 1954.
Colour photographs: Paul Skilleter
Road tests: Courtesy of *Motor*
Printed in England by: J.H.Haynes & Co. Ltd

Titles in the *Super Profile* series

Ariel Square Four (F388)
BMW R69 & R69S (F387)
BSA Bantam (F333)
Honda CB750 sohc (F351)
MV Agusta America (F334)
Norton Commando (F335)
Sunbeam S7 & S8 (F363)
Triumph Trident (F352)
Triumph Thunderbird (F353)

Austin-Healey 'Frogeye' Sprite (F343)
Ferrari 250GTO (F308)
Ford Cortina 1600E (F310)
Ford GT40 (F332)
Fiat X1/9 (F341)
Jaguar E-Type (F370)
Jaguar D-Type & XKSS (F371)
Jaguar Mk 2 Saloons (F307)
Jaguar SS90 & SS100 (F372)
Lancia Stratos (F340)
Lotus Elan (F330)
MGB (F305)
MG Midget & Austin-Healey Sprite (except 'Frogeye') (F344)
Morris Minor & 1000 (ohv) (F331)
Porsche 911 Carrera (F311)
Rolls-Royce Corniche (F411)
Triumph Stag (F342)

B29 Superfortress (F339)
Boeing 707 (F356)
Harrier (F357)
Phantom II (F376)
Sea King (F377)
Super Etendard (F378)

Further titles in this series will be published at regular intervals. For information on new titles please contact your bookseller or write to the publisher.

FOREWORD

'Now and again it happens that circumstances bring a person suddenly into prominence and he or she instantly becomes a favourite in the public affections. Something similar occurs sometimes with new cars and it is likely to happen to the new Morris Minor.'

This prediction, made following the *Autocar* road test of the 1948 Morris Minor Series M.M., undoubtedly proved correct, as the car and its successors did secure a place in the affection of people throughout the world. Even now in the post-production era, as numbers inevitably diminish, the Morris Minor remains a firm favourite.

Much has been done to ensure that Morris Minors will remain part of the motoring scene in the future. Aided by the establishment of specialist firms and by the existence of a large network of owners' clubs throughout the world, the Morris Minor seems destined to outlast many of its more modern counterparts.

This book examines the development of the Morris Minor from its earliest beginnings as a concept in the mind of its creator and designer Alec Issigonis (later Sir Alec), through its various development stages – first as the Mosquito and then as the first production Morris Minor, the Series M.M. The cycle of development from its inception to its eventual demise in favour of the overhead valve (O.H.V.) powered Series II models is fully documented in pictorial form in the Photo Gallery and the major production changes are documented in the Evolution section. For the technically minded, specifications of all Series M.M. models are included and elsewhere the predecessors to the post-war 'Minor' are considered. Contemporary road tests are included and amongst other things provide an additional historical viewpoint to the reception given to what was then a revolutionary vehicle. The joys and pitfalls of buying, owning and restoring a Series M.M. Morris Minor over thirty years after production ceased, are highlighted in the Owners' View and Buying features. Support services in the form of books, specialist firms, and owners' clubs are considered also.

Collecting and researching contemporary material has been an interesting and necessary part of compiling this book. Many people have assisted me in this and I would like to acknowledge the help of: Anders Clausager of B.L. Heritage who provided me with up-to-date statistical information and useful photographic material; the library staff at the National Motor Museum who supplied a wealth of information from their archives; Kim Hearn and Lauren James of *Autocar* who spent a great deal of time researching 'the Series M.M. in motorsport' and *Motor* who permitted the reproduction of contemporary road tests on the Morris Minor Series M.M.

I am particularly grateful to Jack Daniels and Reginald Job for their time and patience in answering my queries about pre-production days and Paul Skilleter who, apart from taking most of the colour photographs in the Photo Gallery, has once again been a source of encouragement in compiling this book. I am indebted to the members of the Morris Minor Owners Club who kindly made their cars available for the photographic session at Hazeley Manor and to Peter Gamble and Michael Hupton in particular for their valuable contributions in ensuring accuracy on a number of technical and historical points.

Finally I would like to acknowledge the assistance of Roy Turner in providing me with a vast selection of photographs and of Sue Hardy who, as always, has been ever patient in the typing of the manuscript of this book.

Ray Newell

HISTORY

Family Tree

When the Morris Minor Series M.M. made its debut at Earls Court, London on the occasion of the 1948 Motor Show it was acclaimed by many as a revolutionary new small car. It carried on the already well established traditions of Morris Motors and along with its stable companions heralded a new era in motoring design and engineering.

The 1948 Motor Show was itself an extra special occasion as it was the first show of its kind to take place in Britain for ten years due to the Second World War. It was a new beginning and it was fitting that the three Morris cars on show should be described by *The Autocar* as 'entirely new'. Nevertheless a sense of British tradition was maintained in the choice of names for the new models. In spite of their innovative nature the Morris Oxford, Morris Six and Morris Minor carried on already familiar Morris names.

'Modern descendant of a famous ancestor' was how *The Autocar* regarded the new Morris Oxford. With its modern lines, unitary construction, independent front suspension, column gearchange and 1476cc side-valve engine, it was a long way from the first 2-seater car which William

Morris produced in 1913 and to which he gave the name Morris Oxford. It was a long way too, from the 'Bullnose' and the 'Flatnose' Oxfords and Cowleys of the '20s which helped launch a career which would see William Morris, later Lord Nuffield, acknowledged as the most successful British car manufacturer of the inter-war years.

The 1948 Morris Six Series M.S. carried on the tradition of 'Sixes', the most successful of which was the 2.5-litre overhead camshaft-engined 1928 model. The post-war version with its 2.2-litre six cylinder overhead camshaft engine shared mechanical and some styling features with the Six Eighty Wolseley which was announced at the same time. It continued in production until 1954 by which time 12,465 had been produced.

Morris Minor was not a new name either. Morris Motors had produced an overhead valve 847cc model called the Morris Minor in 1929, following their takeover of the Wolseley company. The intention was to produce a model to rival the best-selling Austin Seven and thus to secure a foothold in the small-car market. Though the car sold reasonably well it never seriously rivalled the Austin Seven – in spite of a £100 price tag in 1930. The Wolseley-derived overhead camshaft engine, regarded by some as too sophisticated for the Morris Minor, was replaced by a simpler side-valve unit in 1931. This engine remained in use until production ceased in 1934, by which time hydraulic brakes and a four-speed synchromesh gearbox had been introduced. It is interesting to note that the discarded overhead camshaft engine continued to be used in a slightly modified form along with the Morris Minor chassis in the first MG Midget – the M type.

If the first Morris Minor had not attained all the success that had been hoped for, then its post-

war successors were destined to make up for it and put the name Morris firmly in the record books. Few would have predicted in 1948 that the new Morris Minor Series M.M. would be the first stage in a total production run which would span twenty-two years and, in the process, see the Series M.M. and its successors break the million sales barrier for a British car for the first time. In view of this it was perhaps appropriate that it should have been another best selling Morris Car which retained the most direct link with the Morris Minor Series M.M.

The Morris Eight, introduced in 1934, was a popular model and in its first four years of production sales topped a quarter of a million. The 'Eight' was subsequently updated with Series II and Series E models and continued in production until 1948. The Series E was the immediate predecessor to the Morris Minor Series M.M. and a legacy of its production was the well tried and tested 918cc side-valve engine. Following a decision at Morris Motors late in the development programme, a slightly modified version of this engine was selected to power the Series M.M.

While this decision ensured an element of continuity, the emergence of new ideas on body construction was destined to revolutionise British car production techniques in the post-war years. The first indications of the impending changes were embodied in the design of two 1938 cars. The Morris Series M Ten and the Vauxhall Ten Four pioneered new ideas in chassis design. The days of separate chassis frames were numbered and the concept of monocoque construction was soon to be an integral part of British car production.

The impetus for such changes came about as a result of many varied factors. The Nuffield Organisation Publicity Department in reviewing the factors influencing the development of the Morris Minor Series M.M. noted that, "the exceptional smoothness of British roads, the conservative cornering habits of domestic drivers and the fact that fewer than one car in ten was shipped overseas all conspired to produce a climate of opinion in which the public would buy archaic designs of chassis so that standards of comfort then available in America were far ahead of anything to be had in the U.K. and the levels of steering, cornering power and road holding normal in England could not be compared with those established in Europe. For example, when war broke out in 1939 only two British small cars had combined body and chassis construction, only two had independent front wheel suspension, none had both and none had rack and pinion steering''. When one adds to these observations the fact that there was in post-war Britain a need to produce a small, practical, economical family car which would boost export sales, one can see that the Morris Minor Series M.M. was the right car, at the right time, with the right combination of new design features and proven mechanical reliability.

However, the development of the car had begun many years before.

Concept and Design

Alec Issigonis joined Morris Motors in 1936 as part of the design team working on the Series M Ten which went into production in 1938. His brief was to work on the suspension layout and design, but in the event his ideas were not used in the production model.

Nevertheless, they were destined to re-emerge when, in the midst of numerous wartime projects, Issigonis was given the task of designing a new small car for Morris Motors. Assisted by Jack Daniels and later by Reginald Job, Issigonis set about producing what was to be a revolutionary car. Most

of the initial ideas belonged to Issigonis and judging from his early sketches he had very clear ideas from the outset about the sort of small car he wanted. Nothing quite like it had been seen before and many of its features were quite new – even controversial.

The monocoque construction, rack and pinion steering with independent front suspension incorporating torsion bars, and 14 inch road wheels, were all guaranteed to attract attention, even if the striking, sweeping lines of the body design should have failed to do so.

The first prototype incorporating these new ideas and powered by a 6hp engine emerged in 1943. Reginald Job recalls the transformation from concept to reality in the form of the Mosquito.

"As for the styling and design of the bodyshell – I was given a one twelfth scale model of the car as Issigonis wanted it. From that I made a $\frac{1}{4}$ size drawing in order to iron out the various templates taken from the model. Then I made a design layout in linen-backed cartridge paper (full size) and from this the first prototype bodyshell was made and ultimately a car, namely the Mosquito, was produced".

This was just the beginning. As Reginald Job put it, "Issigonis then decided on considerable modifications to the body shape, which I incorporated in a second full size design layout – this time on a painted aluminium sheet 16ftx5ftx16gauge. I think that there was another prototype made to this layout but Issigonis still was not satisfied and so a third completely new layout was made, by me, with various modifications, such as an additional $1\frac{3}{4}$ inch in the width of the waist. I worked out all the shapes in the layout to $\frac{1}{64}$ of an inch by means of what was termed surface development. Using this method you can work out one template shape from another and so on, so that all the shapes flow smoothly from one end of the body

to the other. This was accepted practice then but it is not used now".

Modifications to the design continued and, in all, eight prototypes were produced over a five year period. Some of these were powered by a flat-four water-cooled experimental engine. Jack Daniels and Issigonis favoured this engine design which used a three-speed gearbox with column gear change. 800cc and 1100cc versions were used extensively in trials in the 1947 Mosquito. However the use of a flat-four engine was not confined to this project. At the same time Issigonis had oversight of a continuing experiment to develop a utilitarian military vehicle. The 'Morris Gutty' – an experimental vehicle akin to a jeep – was fitted with a much more powerful flat-four engine capable of producing 40bhp. It suffered from overheating problems and never made it into production.

Interestingly the flat-four engine fitted to the Mosquito suffered the same fate, though not for the same reasons. Jack Daniels recalls that the major problem in developing the smaller version of the flat-four engine was 'inter-factory politics'. At the end of the day the costs of developing a new engine for full scale production were deemed to be too great and so the already well established side-valve engine used by Morris Motors in the Morris 8 Series E went into the final pre-production models in a slightly modified form.

Unbeknown to the 'team' the most radical modification was still to come and it was something of an eleventh hour decision. It was decided that the car was too narrow. All the prototypes had been the same width as the Morris 8 – 57 inches. In an attempt to solve the problem, one of the experimental cars was sawn in half, lengthways, the two halves were then moved apart and set up at different intervals. At 4 inches apart, according to the Nuffield organisation, "Proportion was propitiated and Harmony satisfied".

Reginald Job had the unenviable task of accommodating this extra 4 inches and of checking all the revised sketches. This, as he vividly recalls, involved, "...checking and rechecking many hundreds of dimensions before they were sent to Nuffield Metal Products and the company in Birmingham who made up the full size mahogany models which were viewed by us and then used for 'Rellering' the dies to make the production panels".

This decision had serious implications for the whole design of the car. Apart from the obvious gain in internal dimensions, the main benefit was the increased stability and improved roadholding. Body panels had to be modified and the most noticeable effect the change had was the insertion of a 4 inch flat strip in the centre of the bonnet and the introduction of a 4 inch steel fillet between the bumper blades at the front and rear of the car. These had already gone into production as one piece blades pending the start of production. The only expedient solution was to cut them in half and join them in the middle!

Production

It was with these late changes and as the Morris Minor Series M.M. and not as the Mosquito, that the new model went into production. The first car, a 2 door saloon, was made on the 20th September 1948.

The side-valve engines and corresponding gearboxes fitted to the Series M.M. were made by Morris Engines Ltd of Coventry. The bodyshells comprising 834 different parts were manufactured in Birmingham at Nuffield Metal Products Ltd and final assembly took place at Cowley.

Two models were available at the start of production, the Morris Minor Series M.M. 2 door Saloon and the Morris Minor Series M.M. Tourer. Both proved popular and it

soon became evident that the demand for the new models had been underestimated. Within a year of the first car being produced two new assembly tracks had been laid down at Cowley. The importance of the export market soon became apparent and the requirements of the North American lighting laws forced an early rethink on the design of the front end.

Although home market models continued with the low headlights in the grille panel, changes were being considered for export models within a matter of months of production starting. The earliest photographs showing the raised headlights in the later style wings on production models date from December 1948 and it is believed that only one 'lowlight' model was exported to the U.S.A.

The change in design was not a popular move, particularly with Issigonis who resented it. Reginald Job commenting on this production change, had this to say: "Several attempts were made to modify or update the 'Minor' shape, but we found that it was impossible to do this as it ruined the whole car – the shapes being so closely related to each other. The raising of the headlamps and consequent changes to the front wings was all we got away with".

The only other major production change was the introduction of the 4 door Saloon in October 1950. This welcome addition to the range of cars added a new dimension to the Minor's versatility even though it was only available for export when it was first introduced. It incorporated

many refinements in styling and reverted to using a one-piece bumper; as had been originally planned. Another useful addition was the optional interior heater.

When the Morris Minor Series M.M. made its first public appearance at the Earls Court Motor Show in October 1948 as part of the new range of Morris cars, it created quite a stir. A lot of the advance publicity concentrated on the middle of the range Morris Oxford scheduled for its 'World Premiere' at the show, but in the event the Morris Minor stole the show and created a buzz of excitement in the motoring press. The lavish praise was well justified, for the Morris Minor Series M.M. proved its popularity in the foreign market place.

At home it outshone even its more expensive contemporaries such as the Jowett Javelin and Hillman Minx and as far afield as Australia it was heralded as the new British 'baby car'.

Its size was an important factor in the launch theme. Billed as 'The World's Supreme Small Car' much was made of its compactness and its economy. Its appeal was immediate and glowing compliments on its design and its performance appeared in the Motoring press.

Motor even went so far as to say that "there can be no pretence that it approaches perfection" and that it was "a car which pleases both drivers and passengers alike".

Viewed in this light it is perhaps not so surprising that, with slight body restyling and regular mechanical updates, the Morris Minor enjoyed such a long production run.

Reasons for Discontinuation

The Morris Minor Series M.M. ceased production officially in February 1953. For some time prior to this, however, Series II models fitted with an 803cc engine were manufactured alongside Series M.M. models on the Cowley assembly lines. The series was gradually phased out and, given that the only outward sign of the change from Series M.M. to Series II was a new bonnet badge arrangement and that the only significant change to the bodyshell was the introduction of a curved bulkhead panel, it can be argued that it was not so much discontinued as updated.

The update centred around the M.M.'s one real failing – a lack of power. There was a consensus of opinion that the car was underpowered. Wilson McComb of *Autosport* caught the mood right when he said that all members of the 'Minority' had to admit that, "Their beloved could not be considered a fast lady – or even slightly indiscreet".

At Morris Motors a replacement engine had been under review for some time. An overhead valve version of the 918cc engine already in production had been developed for use in the Wolseley Eight. This engine, capable of 33bhp at 4400rpm, was favoured by the design team and by Jack Daniels in particular for inclusion in the Morris Minor.

At the end of the day, however, organisational changes in the management structure were to prove more influential than engineering acumen.

The main rival to Morris Motors was the Austin Motor Company and the prospect of a merger between these two manufacturing groups seemed remote. A certain amount of animosity existed between the rival groups and so it was with some surprise that the news was received that a merger had been agreed between Lord Nuffield and Leonard Lord in November 1951. The new company, the British Motor Corporation, was a formidable combination.

It was as part of the rationalisation programme that the Austin A series engine, used in the A30, emerged as the successor to the side-valve engine fitted to the Series M.M. Morris Minor. Plans for the 8hp Wolseley O.H.V. 918cc engine to be fitted to the Morris Minor were abandoned.

Motorsport

Anyone who has driven a Series M.M. Morris Minor in standard production form would readily agree that it is an unlikely contender for serious competitive motorsport. The characteristics of good roadholding and positive steering were far outweighed by the M.M.'s sluggish acceleration and relatively low top speed of 62mph. Not surprisingly few successes were ever recorded in international events.

One notable exception was the 1949 Monte Carlo Rally when the all-woman team of Betty Haig, Barbara Marshall and Mrs 'Bill' Wisdom drove their 1948 Series M.M. Saloon, NWL 858, to a creditable second place in the *Coupes Des Dames* and a sixth place in the up to 1000cc class. This success was never repeated even though Series M.M. cars were entered for international rallies like the 'Monte' and the R.A.C. throughout the early fifties. In long distance events the Morris Minor Series M.M. proved its reliability, performing creditably in the U.S.A. in the Alaskan Endurance Trial and at Sebring in the six hour Grand Prix of Endurance in 1950.

Series M.M. saloons and tourers were much more at home in the atmosphere of friendly rivalry which prevailed at club level in the early fifties in the era before stringent competition regulations existed. There were those who added more of a competitive edge to events by equipping their otherwise sedate Series M.M.s with one of the new-fangled conversions marketed at the time.

These included the Derrington Conversion favoured by Stirling Moss and fitted to his own M.M. Saloon to give it 'a bit more steam'. In actual fact the full Derrington conversion, including a 'Silvertop' cylinder head and twin carburettor layout and special plugs, inner valve springs and exhaust valves along with a 'deep note' exhaust system, considerably increased acceleration and produced a top speed of well over 70mph while still retaining good fuel economy.

A further contemporary modification available to boost the performance of the Series M.M. was the Shorrock Supercharger. *Light Car and Cycle* road tested a blown Series M.M. Minor in 1950 and with a supercharger fitted to the standard side-valve engine, recorded an average speed of 76.2mph for a flying quarter mile. Corrected speeds of up to 80mph were recorded and the tester's considered opinion was, "On the open road the Minor at once takes on the characteristics of a sports car. It is rock steady, steers to perfection and its speed rises into the class of vehicles very much larger. Roadholding is exceptionally good and fast cornering is effortless".

At almost £80.00 this was an expensive modification in the 1950s and it is not altogether surprising that the Alta Overhead Conversion marketed by Geoffrey Taylor for about half the price was much more in demand. Developed by Taylor following a successful career in designing and manufacturing Alta $1\frac{1}{2}$-litre and 2-litre racing cars, the Alta Overhead

Conversion for the Morris Minor Series M.M. was intended to be an easy-to-fit conversion which would substantially improve the maximum speed and acceleration times.

Made from 'Birmidal' aluminium alloy with Brico valve seats, the Alta head functioned well with a single carburettor set up and on test returned an average maximum speed of 76.5mph and greatly improved acceleration times. (See Road Test section).

The improved performance gained from fitting the Alta O.H.V. conversion was evident for all to see in the performances of Alan Foster's 'lowlight' Series M.M. which was raced regularly with some creditable success in the early '50s in Britain. Australian owners of Series M.M. Morris Minors had the additional option of selecting a 'home produced' conversion. Monaro Motors, specialists in Morris Minor and MG tuning based in Melbourne, produced a twin carburettor kit which, along with a special Burgess-type silencer with a $\frac{3}{16}$ in oversize diameter tail pipe, considerably increased overall performance.

Success Review

Viewed objectively, the Morris Minor Series M.M. was a success by virtue of the fact that it was representative of a new era in terms of motoring design and engineering. The fact that it was the first of a total of five 'Series' of models, which together spanned a production run of twenty-two years and encompassed the manufacture of 1.6 million vehicles, says something for the esteem in which the vehicles were held and does credit to the original design team. That they 'got it right' is indisputable.

In terms of total market sales, the actual production run of just over 176,000 Series M.M.s was not earth-shattering. However it did sell better than its stablemates, the Oxford and the 'Six' launched at the same time, and given that over 125,000 of the Series M.M.s were exported, it can be said that they contributed substantially to the successful export drive in the post-war years. In fact Canada, Australia, New Zealand, U.S.A., South Africa, India, Holland and Eire were on the export list at Morris Motors.

The continuing interest in Series M.M. models today and their increasing status as collectors' cars is indicative of their durability and their long-standing appeal. Amidst the thought of success, however, there is a nagging feeling of what might have been.

What if the Series M.M. had had a more powerful engine?

Would the success in motorsport have exceeded the grand total of one good international showing? What if the Wolseley O.H.V. engine had been fitted to the Series M.M. prior to the Austin-Morris merger? What if the home market demand for the cars could have been supplied as well as the export quotas?

The Series M.M. had the potential for greater success in its own right but it will probably be remembered as part of the overall success of Morris Minor production 1948-71.

EVOLUTION

During the course of production two types of identification plate were used on Series M.M. vehicles. The early type which contained a model/type code, the car number and the engine number was used until April 1952. After this time a more detailed car number code was used along with the engine number. Both plates were mounted on the right hand side of the dash, in the engine bay next to the main wiring harness grommet aperture.

The model/type identification code used on the early type plate for Series M.M. Morris Minors was MNR. An additional code was added to this depending upon the paint finish used. For cars finished in synthetic paint the letters SYN were used, while for cars finished in Synobel the symbol S was used. Cars finished in cellulose enamel were not marked in any way.

The car (chassis) number, which was stamped on the body, also appeared on the identification plate prefixed by the letters SMM.

The engine number, which appears on a metal disc secured to the cylinder block casting, was also put on the identification plate for easy reference.

Thus a car with the following information on the identification plate : MNR/SYN, SMM1125, Engine No. 1324, could be identified as a Morris Minor Series

M.M., finished in synthetic paint, Car No. 1125, Engine No. 1324.

From April 1952 car (chassis) numbers were prefixed by a new and more detailed identification code consisting of three letters and two numbers. The first letter indicates the make and model (F = Morris Minor); the second letter indicates the body type (A = 4 door saloon, B = 2 door saloon, C = tourer); the third letter indicates the colour in which the vehicle is finished (e.g., A = Black, B = Grey); the first number indicates the class to which the vehicle belongs (e.g., I = R.H.D. Home Market, 2 = R.H.D. Export, 4 = North America); the second number indicates the type of paint used to finish the vehicle (e.g., I = Synthetic, 2 = Synobel, 3 = Cellulose). Thus FCB13 = Morris Minor Tourer produced for the home market and finished in grey cellulose paint.

There were eight pre-production prototype 'Morris Minors'. The first of these was the 'Mosquito' which was built in December 1943. The first Morris Minor was built on September 20th 1948 and was allocated Car Number 501. Subsequent changes and developments for Series M.M. cars are listed below. It should be noted that the change points are, in some cases, approximate, as the manufacturer sometimes incorporated modifications before or after the official change point. The earliest recorded official change point is given in each case and where possible R.H.D. and L.H.D. car numbers are given.

A comprehensive list of R.H.D. car numbers is also included for numbers used at the beginning of each quarter year during production *i.e., 1st January, April, July, October.

501 R.H.D.: First Series M.M. 2 door saloon 20th September 1948.
904 R.H.D./5600 L.H.D.: Front suspension modified. Fork to lower arm strengthened.
1243 R.H.D.: *1st January 1949.*
5708 L.H.D.: First export car fitted with highlamp wings. Marked U.S.A. in records.
3389 R.H.D./6142 L.H.D.: Flush fitting circular rear light units incorporating stop lamps introduced. American models used pedestal type mounting.
Engine No. 3827: Modified speedometer drive assembly introduced with new oil seal and double hexagon.
4591 R.H.D.: *1st April 1949.*
16810 R.H.D.: Seat adjustment modified; carpet altered.
17580 R.H.D./7967 L.H.D.: Triangular profile helmet type rear stop tail light units fitted.
17840 R.H.D./8700 L.H.D.: Rear spring front mounting modified. Renewable bush plates fitted.
18083 R.H.S./8888 L.H.D.: Sealing rubbers introduced for window regulator channel.
18491 R.H.D.: *1st July 1949.*
18885 R.H.D.: Door sealing rubbers changed. Sorbo replaced by moquette-covered clip-on type.
26061: *1st October 1949.*
26102 R.H.D./10607 L.H.D.: Windscreen rubber channel, screen, centre pillar and weather strip modified. Inside moulding discontinued.
27384 R.H.D./10006 L.H.D.: Bottom radiator hose arrangement changed. Metal pipe and two-hose arrangement replaced by single bellows type hose.
29862 R.H.D./11958 L.H.D.: Steering modified. Steering lever taper enlarged.

(Researched by A.D. Clausager and incorporated courtesy of B.L. Heritage Ltd.)

31782 R.H.D./12324 L.H.D.: Door surround/top painted instead of chrome.
31790 R.H.D./12338 L.H.D.: Front hub and stub shaft modified.
33241 R.H.D./12869 L.H.D.: Bonnet chain and fixing discontinued.
33375 R.H.D.: *1st January 1950.*
34490 R.H.D./13251 L.H.D.: Boot lock striker plate modified.
38471 R.H.D. Fascia controls identified by letters on pull switches.
40835 R.H.D./43554 L.H.D.: Rear screen rubber and fittings changed. Inner moulding discontinued.
46415 R.H.D.: *1st April 1950.*
57587 R.H.D.: *1st July 1950.*
57681 R.H.D./54349 L.H.D.: Two sun visors fitted as standard. 2 door saloon available in grey and beige colours.
62551 R.H.D.: 4 door saloon introduced 5th September 1950.
65004 L.H.D.: Specification included new 'high' lamp wings. Separate side lights in revised grille panel, 7" headlamps. Stainless steel window surrounds, chrome finisher on rear window rubber, door escutcheons, one piece bumper valence and blade front and rear and two wipers. Interior innovations included strap type door pulls, interior light, arm rests on rear doors, self-cancelling trafficators, demister ducts on fascia and ashtrays in front door panels.
63541 R.H.D./64813 L.H.D.: Maroon carpet and maroon piping for hood cover (Tourer) discontinued.
63541 R.H.D./68068 L.H.D.: Wing piping in Maroon, Platinum Grey and Romain Green discontinued.
63542 R.H.D./65069 L.H.D.: Wing piping introduced in Thames Blue, Gascoyne Grey and Mist Green.
63829 R.H.D.: *1st October 1950.* Engine No. 63276
65736 R.H.D.: Oil filter fitted. Oil pump & sump modified. Window ventilator assembly changed. New style catch fitted. 2 door saloon and

tourer (same as 4 door saloon).
69622 R.H.D./71098 L.H.D.: 2 door saloon and tourer fitted with strap type door pulls with Chromium plated finisher.
69962 R.H.D./71222 L.H.D.: Petrol filler neck modified.
72985 R.H.D.: Increase to two wipers for home market, 2 door saloon and tourer.
78235 R.H.D./73748 L.H.D.: Radiator top hose modified.
78593 R.H.D./73961 L.H.D.: Accelerator cable assembly modified. Engine No. 77001: 'Minor' changes to dynamo mounting bracket, exhaust manifold, carburettor and air silencer/cleaner. Impeller type water pump fitted. Heater available as option on home market models. Fitted as standard on U.S.A. models.
79783 R.H.D.: *1st January 1951.*
83204 R.H.D./81501 L.H.D.: Split bumper and fillet discontinued. One piece valance and bumper blade introduced 2 door saloon.
83390 R.H.D./81595 L.H.D.: New type 'high' headlamp front wings fitted along with new grille panel with side lights. Chromium plated grille insert retained.
90117 R.H.D./89726 L.H.D.: Painted radiator grille introduced. Chromium plated grille available as an option March 1951. Plain painted hub caps introduced to replace chromium plated ones March 1951. (Painted hub caps with 'M' motif later made available in black).

90318 R.H.D./89910 L.H.D.: Brake shoe assembly front and rear modified.
90398 R.H.D.: *1st April 1951.*
90685 R.H.D./93454 L.H.D.: Over-riders fitted to bumper assembly 4 door saloon.
91982 R.H.D./99332 L.H.D.: Shock absorbers pivot arm to upper link modified.
100920 R.H.D./102836 L.H.D.: Tourer redesignated convertible. Fixed rear side windows on tourer introduced. Detachable side screen discontinued. Hood sticks increased to five and tension wires fitted.
106124 R.H.D.: *1st July 1951.*
109699 R.H.D./110504 L.H.D.: Bonnet changed. New style hinges and buffer to dash and body side introduced August 1951.
114502 R.H.D./110631 L.H.D.: Trafficator switch mounting bracket discontinued (4 door saloon).
114122 R.H.D./110707 L.H.D.: Rear screen chrome finisher discontinued 4 door saloon. September 1951. Chrome hub caps reintroduced with 'M' motif.
114924 R.H.D./110813 L.H.D.: Front suspension top link modified.
116618 R.H.D.: *1st October 1951.*
123567 R.H.D./122232 L.H.D.: Tourer hood canopy changed. Tension wires discontinued.
124810 R.H.D./122788 L.H.D.: Ashtray fitted to fascia grille 2 door saloon and tourer.
127712 R.H.D.: *1st January 1952.*
131461 R.H.D./126598 L.H.D.: Ashtrays discontinued in door panels, 4 door saloon. Introduced in fascia grille.
131858 R.H.D./126725 L.H.D.: Hub and brake drum modified.
139175 R.H.D./138415 L.H.D.: Headlamp beam warning light fitted, 4 door saloon.
139360 R.H.D./139513 L.H.D.: Glove locker badge changed. Metal badge replaced by plastic one.
139439 R.H.D.: *1st April 1952.* New type identification plate used. R.H.D. and L.H.D. car numbers no longer allocated in batches.

140823 R.H.D.: Headlamp beam warning light fitted, 2 door saloon and tourer.

144454 R.H.D./144408 L.H.D.: Secondary steering rack damper fitted.

149078 R.H.D.: Thames Blue wing piping discontinued.

149079 R.H.D.: Clarendon Grey wing piping introduced. Steering column bracket support fitted.

151649 R.H.D.: *1st July 1952.*

151844 R.H.D.: Birch Grey wing piping discontinued. Mist Green wing piping discontinued.

151845 R.H.D.: Empire Green wing piping introduced.

159190 R.H.D.: First C.K.D. (completely knocked down) vehicle with O.H.V. engine.

160001 R.H.D.: Series M.M. side valve models and Series II O.H.V. models, begin production side by side.

163401 R.H.D.: *1st October 1952.*

175544 R.H.D.: *1st January 1953.*

176410: Final Car No. 4 door saloon Series M.M.

177640 R.H.D.: Maroon wing piping re-introduced.

179820: Final Car No. tourer Series M.M.

179839: Final Car No. 2 door saloon Series M.M.

Footnote: Final Series M.M. built 23rd February 1953.

Note: The type of paint used on Morris Minor Series M.M. cars changed early on during production. Prior to Car Nos. 2117 R.H.D., 5855 L.H.D. (2 door saloons) and 3871 R.H.D., 6255 L.H.D. (tourers), vehicles were finished in cellulose. Cars after this were finished in Synobel or synthetic. The identification procedure has already been outlined in this Section.

As Series M.M. vehicles were finished with matching wing piping, the references to the introduction and discontinuation of wing piping colours serve as useful indicators to the official body colour change points. Upon its introduction the Series M.M. was available in three colours, Black, Romain Green and Platinium Grey. Maroon was introduced late in 1948 but was later discontinued because of its tendency to fade.

SPECIFICATION

Please note that the specifications relate to each of the models upon their introduction.
For production changes see 'Evolution'.

Type   Morris Minor Series M.M.

Built   Cowley, England, 1948 – 53
                            Total number built, 176,002

Engine   Designated type U.S.H.M.2
                            Cast iron block and head. Four cylinders, in line, side-valve
   Capacity: 918.636cc (56.06cu in)
   Bore & Stroke: 57mm x 90mm
   Compression: 6.5/6.7:1
   Maximum Power: 27.5bhp at 4,400rpm
   Maximum Torque: 39lb/ft at 2,400rpm
   Carburettor: S.U. Horizontal type H1
   Fuel Pump: S.U. Type L
   Air Cleaner: Dry gauze type (Home Market)
                            Oil bath type (Export Market)

Transmission   Rear wheel drive from front mounted engine.
                            4-speed gearbox bolted to rear engine plate. Synchromesh on 2nd, 3rd
                            and top gears. Clutch, Borg and Beck $6\frac{1}{4}$ inch (158.7mm) dry plate Type
                            AG.
                            Gear ratios: Reverse 3.95:1, First 3.95:1, Second 2.30:1, Third 1.54:1,
                            Top 1.00:1. Final Drive: Semi Floating Hypoid axle. 9:41 (normal) 7x37
                            (special), 8/43 axle. Final Drive ratio: 4.55:1 (normal), 5.286:1 (special),
                            5.375:1 (8/43). Overall Gear ratios: *Normal;* Reverse 17.994:1, First
                            17.994:1, Second 10.477:1, Third 7.015:1, Fourth 4.55:1. *Special;*
                            Reverse 20.878:1, First 20.878:1, Second 12.157:1. Third 8.140:1,
                            Fourth 5.286:1. 8/43 Axle; Reverse 21.23:1, First 21.23:1, Second
                            12.36:1, Third 8.20:1, Fourth 5.375:1.

Wheelbase and Track   Wheelbase 7ft 2in (218.44cm)
                            Track: Front 4ft $2\frac{5}{8}$in (1284cm), Rear 4ft $2\frac{5}{16}$in (1278cm)

Suspension   Front: Independent by torsion bars and links. Armstrong Double Acting

Hydraulic Dampers.
Rear: Semi elliptic leaf springs. Armstrong Double Acting Hydraulic Dampers.

Steering

Rack and Pinion, 2.6 turns lock-to-lock
Turning Circle, R.H. 33ft 1in (10.09m)
L.H. 32ft 11in (10.04m)

Brakes

Lockhead Hydraulic 7in diameter drums (17.8cm)
Front: two leading shoes
Rear: one leading and one trailing shoe.

Wheels and Tyres

14in (35cm) pressed steel disc. 4 bolt fixings. Tyres, 5.00x14

Bodywork

Designed by Issigonis, unitary all-steel construction. Assembled at Cowley. Upon introduction 2 door 'Saloon' and 'Tourer' models available. 4 door saloon introduced later. See 'Evolution'.

Dimensions and Weight

2 door saloon ($15\frac{1}{2}$ cwt)
Tourer (14cwt)
4 door saloon ($15\frac{3}{4}$cwt)

	Overall width	Overall height	Overall length
2 door saloon	5ft 1in (155cm)	5ft 0in (152cm)	12ft 4in (376cm)
Tourer	5ft 1in (155cm)	4ft 9in (143cm)	12ft 4in (376cm)
4 door saloon	5ft 1in (155cm)	5ft 0in (152cm)	12ft 4in (376cm)

Ground clearance all models $6\frac{3}{4}$in (17.1cm)

Electrical System

Positive earth, 12volt, 38amp/hr battery, Lucas G.T.W. 7A/1. Mounted on tray in engine bay. Lucas dynamo type C39PV with Lucas compensated voltage control box and coil ignition.
Headlamps: 5in Lucas, single dip (home market models), double dip (export models). 36/36 watt.
Pilot lights 6 watts
Semaphore trafficators 3 watts.

Performance

4 door Saloon. Maximum speed 60.1mph.
Maximum speed in gears; First 24mph, Second 37mph, Third 50mph.
Acceleration: 0-30 mph 10 secs, 0-40mph 17.2 secs, 0-50 37.1 secs.
Standing $\frac{1}{4}$ mile 27.6 secs.
Fuel consumption 36-40mpg.

The Motor

February 16, 1949.

The Motor Road Test No. 4/49 ——————

Make: Morris   **Type:** Minor
Makers: Morris Motors Ltd., Cowley, Oxford

Dimensions and Seating

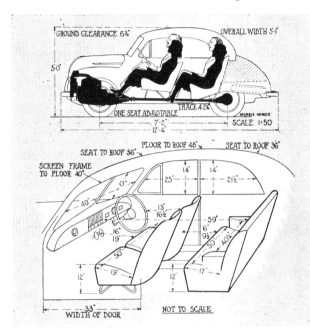

In Brief

Price £280 plus purchase tax £78 10s. 7d.
equals £358 10s. 7d.
Capacity .. .. .. 919 c.c.
Road weight unladen .. 15¼ cwt.
Front/rear weight distribution 56/44
Laden weight as tested .. 18¾ cwt.
Fuel consumption . 40.5 m.p.g.
Maximum speed .. . 62.3 m.p.h.
Maximum speed on 1 in 20
gradient .. .. 36 m.p.h.
Maximum top-gear gradient 1 in 16
Acceleration, 10-30 on top 17.6 secs.
0-50 through gears 24.2 secs.
Gearing : 14.9 m.p.h. in top at 1,000
r.p.m. 63 m.p.h. at 2,500 ft. per
minute piston speed.

Specification

Engine

Cylinders	..	..	4
Bore	..	..	57 mm.
Stroke	..	..	90 mm.
Cubic capacity	..	..	919 c.c.
Piston area	..	..	15.8 sq. ins.
Valves	..	..	Side
Compression ratio	..	..	6.6 to 1
Max. power	..	..	27 b.h.p.
at	..	..	4,400 r.p.m.
B.h.p. per sq. in. piston area			1.71
Piston speed at max. b.h.p.	..	2,600 ft./min.
Carburetter	..	..	S.U. horizontal
Ignition	..	..	Coil
Sparking plugs	..	14 mm. Champion L.10
Fuel pump	..	..	S.U. electric
Oil filter	..	..	—

Transmission

Clutch	..	..	Borg & Beck 6¼-in.
Top gear	..	..	4.55
3rd gear	..	..	7.01
2nd gear	..	..	10.48
1st gear	..	..	17.99
Propeller shaft	..	..	Hardy Spicer
Final drive	..	..	Hypoid bevel

Chassis

Brakes	..	..	Lockheed hydraulic
Brake drum diameter	..	..	7 ins.
Friction lining area	..	67.2 sq. ins.
Tyres	..	..	Dunlop 5.00×14
Suspension	..	Torsion bar I.F.S. and semi-elliptic rear springs
Steering gear	..	..	Rack and pinion

Performance factors (At laden weight as tested)

Piston area, sq. ins. per ton	..	16.9
Brake lining area, sq. ins. per ton	..	72
Litres per ton-mile	.. ..	1,970

Fully described in "The Motor,"
October 27, 1948

Test Conditions

Cold, slight breeze, dry concrete surface. Pool petrol.

Test Data

ACCELERATION TIMES on Two Upper Ratios

	Top	3rd
10-30 m.p.h.	17.6 secs.	10.2 secs.
20-40 m.p.n.	19.3 secs.	12.1 secs.
30-50 m.p.h.	24.1 secs	—

ACCELERATION TIMES Through Gears

0-30 m.p.h.	8.7 secs.
0-40 m.p.h.	15.1 secs.
0-50 m.p.h.	24.2 secs.
Standing quarter-mile	26.3 secs.

MAXIMUM SPEEDS
Flying Quarter-mile
Mean of four opposite runs .. 62.3 m.p.h.
Best time equals .. .. 64.3 m.p.h.
Speed in Gears
Max. speed in 3rd gear .. .. 50 m.p.h.
Max. speed in 2nd gear .. .. 32 m.p.h.

BRAKES at 30 m.p.h.

0.35 g (= 86 ft. stopping distance) with 25 lb. pedal pressure.
0.87 g (= 34½ ft. stopping distance) with 50 lb. pedal pressure.
0.94 g (= 32 ft. stopping distance) with 75 lb. pedal pressure.
1.00 g (= 30 ft. stopping distance) with 85 lb. pedal pressure.

FUEL CONSUMPTION

Overall consumption for 568 miles, 14 gallons,
equals 40.5 m.p.g.
61.0 m.p.g. at constant 20 m.p.h.
56.0 m.p.g. at constant 30 m.p.h.
50.0 m.p.g. at constant 40 m.p.h.
44.0 m.p.g. at constant 50 m.p.h.
37.0 m.p.g. at constant 60 m.p.h.

STEERING

Left-hand lock, 35 ft.
Right-hand lock, 31 ft.
2¾ turns of steering wheel, lock to lock.

HILL CLIMBING

Max. top-gear speed on 1 in 20 .. 36 m.p.h.
Max. gradient climbable on top gear, 1 in 16 (Tapley 140 lb. per ton).
Max. gradient climbable on 3rd gear, 1 in 9¼ (Tapley 230 lb. per ton).
Max. gradient climbable on 2nd gear, 1 in 7¼ (Tapley 310 lb. per ton).

Maintenance

Fuel tank: 5 gallons. **Sump:** 6¼ pints, S.A.E. 30. **Gearbox :** 1½ pints, S.A.E. 140 gear oil. **Rear axle :** 1½ pints, Hypoid oil. **Radiator :** 13¼ pints. **Chassis lubrication:** 9 grease-gun points. **Ignition timing :** T.D.C. (on full retard). **Spark plug gap:** .018-.022 in. **Contact breaker gap :** .010-.012 in. **Tappets :** inlet .017-.018 in., exhaust .017-.018 in. **Front wheel toe-in:** Parallel. **Camber angle:** Nil. **Caster angle:** 3°. **Tyre pressures :** Front, 24 lb. Rear, 24 lb. **Brake fluid:** Lockheed Orange. **Shock absorber fluid:** Armstrong Piston-type. **Battery :** 12-volt 38 amp./hour. **Lamp bulbs :** Head lamps: left-hand, double-filament 36/36-watt.; right-hand, 36-watt. Pilot lamps, 6-watt. Stop lamp, 6-watt. Trafficators, 3-watt. Panel, side, tail and warning lights, 2.4-watt.

Ref. B/10/49.

February 16, 1949.

The**Motor**

————THE MORRIS MINOR

An Attractive Newcomer Which Sets High Standards of Small-car Stability, Comfort and Economy

PROPORTION.— The roominess of the new car has been combined with aesthetically and aerodynamically satisfactory lines.

RESTRAINED OR-NAMENTATION.— Front-end treatment, in the modern manner, is clean and restrained and the headlamps provide a far better driving light than their low mounting would suggest.

A MONGST the record number of visitors to the Earls Court motor exhibition last October there were many who felt that the new Morris Minor " Stole the Show." It certainly aroused tremendous interest, and while the present trend among rival manufacturers is towards increased engine sizes, there yet remains a big field for a really good and modern small car which is still an " eight."

Our test report on this important 1949 model must be regarded as very much of a composite affair—not merely in that, as is our usual practice, it represents the agreed views of several drivers, but also because it is based on big mileages totalling considerably over a thousand in two distinct cars.

To-day's Prescription

Everyone who drove either of the cars which have passed through our hands agreed that the Minor is a very good 8 h.p. car indeed. There can be no pretence that it approaches perfection, but it is a car which pleases both driver and passengers, and which will almost exactly fulfil the requirements of tens of thousands of motorists in this country and abroad—there has been nothing like it offered in the economy car class previously.

The performance figures reproduced on the opposite page are so exceptionally good, especially in regard to the combination of rapid acceleration through the gears with notable economy, that we do not doubt that they will be regarded with suspicion in certain quarters. They represent the precise figures obtained after a few hundred miles driving on the better of the two cars which have passed through our hands, and although the other model which had done 5,000 hard miles without attention showed inferior speed and economy, the reported figures

obviously are representative of a Minor in the pink of condition running on ordinary Pool petrol.

The published figures, when compared with those obtained on the Series E 1939 Model Morris 8 h.p., closely confirm the designer's claims that streamlining has produced an extra 4-5 m.p.h. of top speed, that a fractional weight saving has made slightly higher gearing acceptable, and that in sum there is a definite advance in fuel economy. On test, the new car shows top- and third-gear acceleration fractionally inferior to that of its predecessor, but is 4.3 m.p.h. faster and is, indeed, notably economical.

It is only by the smallest of margins that the Morris Minor fails to be the most economical post-war car which has been tested by " The Motor." Its figures have only been bettered, however, by slower and smaller cars which, meritorious though they were, attained low weight through very sparse furnishing. A consumption of 61 m.p.g. at 20 m.p.h. represents the extreme of dawdling, but 50 m.p.g. can certainly be obtained by the gentle driver. Even the less economical of the two test cars which was frankly " off colour " could not quite be dragged down to 40 m.p.g., covering 568 miles of performance

testing and really hasty travel at an average of 40.5 m.p.g.

Reasonably high gear ratios contribute to the economy of running which this car features, and also make for very effortless fast cruising on open roads. It is usual to settle down to a steady 50 m.p.h., which speed leaves a pleasant reserve of power for hill-climbing, but if more speed is used and long distances are covered at over 40 m.p.h. averages the car does not protest or hint that it is being over-driven.

Gears to be Used

On the debit side, the high axle ratio gives top-gear acceleration of only moderate briskness. A brief experience of the car might suggest that this lack of " snap " in the highest gear was a major disadvantage, but experience proves that it is not so—because plenty of extra punch is so willingly on call if the gearbox is used, and because a compact, well-sprung and very controllable car is surprisingly seldom slowed by road conditions.

The engine is not entirely silent, but such noise as it makes can fairly be described as a contented hum. The gearbox, however, is entirely silent, as judged from inside the car, even at third-gear speeds approaching 50 m.p.h.

Minor Road Test—Contd.

Indirect ratios have apparently been well chosen except for the lazy driver, who is not encouraged to start from rest in second gear; the gear change is pleasantly smooth and requires little effort, although we felt that a rather longer lever would have been more convenient.

Qualities going to make up roadworthiness are the really striking characteristics of the Minor. It is easy to excuse suspension shortcomings on a small car as resulting from small dimensions—the Minor certainly is small in overall dimensions, but it nevertheless contrives to offer a magnificently level ride, the springs tending slightly towards firmness but yet giving really effective shock insulation at high speeds or low.

Exceptional Stability

Comfort has been allied to very remarkable safe handling characteristics. On the straight there is complete stability, yet there is also quick response to the steering on corners; brisk negotiation of a cross-roads roundabout is simply a matter of right-wrist movement, with no need to use two hands on the wheel. While it would not be accurate to say that there is no roll on corners, the amount is astonishingly small, even if the car is pushed to the limit—a limit at which many sports models would have to give best to this little touring car.

Perhaps the most sensitive tests of riding qualities are for a passenger to write and sleep in the car. By the former test, the Minor is a fraction too firmly sprung to score the highest marks, but by the latter test it gained a very high rating even while covering an astonishing distance within an hour.

There are a great many more points about the car which fully deserve praise, among them the roominess of the four-

REAR DETAILS.—The luggage locker is capacious and includes a separate shelf for the spare wheel, a prop being provided to hold the lid open when required. The off-side rear lamp is matched by a near-side red reflector, a separate lamp illuminating the number plate.

seater body and its luggage locker, and the sensible way in which rear-seat squab and the front passenger seat can be folded away if bulky overloads are to be carried. On the other hand, although the front bucket seats give good support on either side of the hips, the squabs slope back at an angle which is comfortable for a passenger but not for the driver, and the range of driving-seat adjustment cannot cope with any-one more than 6 ft. tall.

Controls generally are quite convenient, although the pedals are perhaps rather closely spaced and the need for a longer gear lever has been mentioned. Visibility, over the short bonnet and all around the car, is excellent save for two points—rounded corners on the V-screen limit a tall driver's lateral vision, and in wet weather the lack of a second wiper blade is felt rather acutely.

The car is pleasantly trimmed inter-

nally, but there are various items of equipment lacking which, although excusable on a £280 car, will doubtless soon be offered as extras by accessory merchants. In standard form, the car has no interior light or rear blind, proves to be protected very well from all engine warmth, and has a rather inaccessible trafficator switch incorporating a warning light instead of the usual self-cancelling mechanism.

Good points on a very smart-looking car include head lamps which are very much better than their low mounting would suggest, even if the dipped beam is so short as to call for marked slowing from an otherwise high night-cruising speed; the interior of the bonnet is illuminated by the parking light bulbs, a practical feature matching the very much-improved engine accessibility of this new model. The luggage locker incorporates a proper shelf accommodating the spare wheel and a comprehensive tool roll, and there is a wide shelf below the facia panel as well as a locker alongside the instrument panel.

Of the clearly calibrated speedometer, we can only say that the two cars with which we have covered big mileages had very different instruments. One had the amount of optimism which we have sadly come to expect on modern cars, roughly 7 per cent., the other gave readings so palpably unrelated to actual m.p.h. that it was only at 10 m.p.h. that the exaggeration came within 20 per cent.

The Morris Minor is an astonishing car, in that one criticizes freely yet would not dream of condemning—its faults are criticized because, when a small car offers merits normally associated with large and expensive models plus a charm of its own, there is inevitably a " much would have more " seeking after costly trimmings. The highest tribute to the Minor is that a variety of drivers hitherto enthusing over larger and faster cars suddenly began to feel that this grown-up baby could fulfil all their requirements and double their m.p.g. figures. The real lament is that, ideally suited though it is to home needs, most of the new Minors will obviously go to keen buyers abroad.

INTELLIGENT SIMPLICITY —Controls for lights, starter and choke are set centrally, with instruments on one hand and a cubby on the other. The cubby lid is released by a press-button which matches the ignition warning lamp, and is supplemented by a full-width parcel shelf.

Super Profile

The Motor Road Test No. 13/50——

Make: Morris   **Type**: Minor Tourer

Makers: Morris Motors Ltd., Cowley, Oxford

Dimensions and Seating

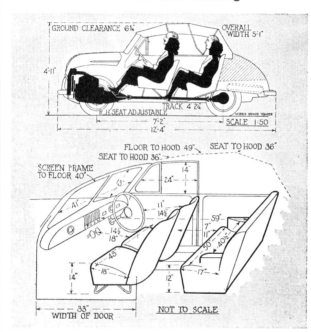

In Brief

Price £299 plus purchase tax £83 16s 1d.
  equals £382 16s. 1d.

Capacity	918.6 c.c.
Unladen kerb weight	14½ cwt.
Fuel consumption	42 m.p.g.
Maximum speed	58.7 m.p h.
Maximum speed on 1 in 20 gradient	37 m.p.h.
Maximum top gear gradient	1 in 18

Acceleration:

10-30 m.p.h. in top	18.2 secs.
0-50 m.p.h. through gears	29.2 secs.

Gearing:
14.9 m.p.h. in top at 1,000 r.p.m.
63 m.p.h. at 2,500 ft. per min.
piston speed.

Specification

Engine

Cylinders	4
Bore	57 mm.
Stroke	90 mm.
Cubic capacity	918.6 c.c.
Piston area	15.8 sq. ins.
Valves	side
Compression ratio	6.6 : 1
Max. power	27 b.h.p.
at	4,400 r.p.m.
Piston speed at max. b.h.p.	2,600 ft. per min.
Carburetter	S U horizontal
Ignition	Lucas coil
Sparking plugs	14 mm. Champion L10
Fuel pump	S.U. electric

Transmission

Clutch	Borg and Beck s.d.p.
Top gear (s/m)	4.55
3rd gear (s/m)	7.015
2nd gear (s/m)	10.477
1st gear	17.994
Propeller shaft	Hardy Spicer, open
Final drive	9/41 Hypoid bevel

Chassis

Brakes	Lockheed hydraulic (2 l.s. front)
Brake drum diameter	7 ins.
Friction lining area	67.2 sq. ins.

Suspension :

Front	Torsion bar and wishbone I.F.S.
Rear	Semi-elliptic leaf springs
Shock absorbers	Armstrong hydraulic
Tyres	Dunlop 5.00 × 14

Steering

Steering gear	Rack and pinion
Turning circle	31 ft.
Turns of steering wheel, lock to lock	2⅓

Performance factors (at laden weight as tested)

Piston area, sq. ins. per ton	17.6
Brake lining area, sq. ins. per ton	75
Specific displacement, litres per ton mile	2,055

Fully described in " The Motor," October 27, 1948.

Test Conditions

Warm, dry weather with light cross wind; smooth tarmac surface; Pool petrol.
Car tested with hood and sidescreens erected.

Test Data

ACCELERATION TIMES on Two Upper Ratios

	Top	3rd
10-30 m.p.h.	18.2 secs.	11.1 secs.
20-40 m.p.h.	21.3 secs.	13.1 secs.
30-50 m.p.h.	28.6 secs.	21.4 secs.

ACCELERATION TIMES Through Gears

0-30 m.p.h.	8.7 secs.
0-40 m.p.h.	15.9 secs.
0-50 m.p.h.	29.2 secs.
Standing quarter-mile	27.1 secs.

MAXIMUM SPEEDS

Flying Quarter-mile

Mean of four opposite runs	58.7 m.p.h.
Best time equals	60.0 m.p.h.

Speed in Gears

Max. speed in 3rd gear	50 m.p.h.
Max. speed in 2nd gear	36 m.p.h.

FUEL CONSUMPTION

54.0 m.p.g. at constant 20 m.p.h.
58.0 m.p.g. at constant 30 m.p.h.
50.0 m.p.g. at constant 40 m.p.h.
41.5 m.p.g. at constant 50 m.p.h.
Overall consumption for 210 miles, 5
gallons = 42.0 m.p.g.

WEIGHT

Unladen kerb weight	14½ cwt.
Front/rear weight distribution	57/43
Weight laden as tested	18 cwt.

INSTRUMENTS

Speedometer at 30 m.p.h.	7% fast
Speedometer at 60 m.p.h.	8% fast
Distance recorder	5% fast

HILL CLIMBING (at steady speeds)

Max. top-gear speed on 1 in 20	37 m.p.h.
Max. gradient on top gear	1 in 18 (Tapley 125 lb./ton)
Max. gradient on 3rd gear	1 in 10.6 (Tapley 210 lb./ton)
Max. gradient on 2nd gear	1 in 7.8 (Tapley 285 lb./ton)

BRAKES AT 30 m.p.h.

0.93 g. retardation (= 32¼ ft. stopping distance) with 150 lb. pedal pressure.
0.86 g. retardation (= 35 ft. stopping distance) with 100 lb. pedal pressure.
0.54 g. retardation (= 56 ft. stopping distance) with 50 lb. pedal pressure.
0.22 g. retardation (= 137 ft. stopping distance) with 25 lb pedal pressure.

Maintenance

Fuel tank: 5 gallons. **Sump**: 6¼ pints, S.A.E. 30. **Gearbox**: 1¼ pints, S.A.E. 90 gear oil. **Rear Axle**: 1½ pints S.A.E. 90 E.P. gear oil. **Steering gear**: S.A.E. 90 gear oil. **Radiator**: 13¼ pints (1 drain tap). **Chassis lubrication**: By grease gun every 500 miles to 9 points. **Firing order**: 1, 3, 4, 2. **Ignition timing**: T.D.C. static. **Spark-plug gap**: 0.018—0.022 in. **Contact breaker gap**: 0.012 in. **Valve timing**: Inlet opens 8° before T.D.C.; Inlet closes 52° after B.D.C.; Exhaust opens 52° before B.D.C.; Exhaust closes 20° after T.D.C. **Tappet clearances** (hot): Inlet and exhaust 0.017 in. **Front wheel toe-in**: ³/₃₂ in. **Camber angle**: Nil. **Castor angle**: 3°. **Tyre pressures**: Front 22 lb., rear 22/24 lb. **Brake fluid**: Lockheed Orange (Overseas, Lockheed No. 5). **Battery**: 12-volt, 38 amp./hour. **Lamp bulbs**: Headlamps, N.S. 36/36 watt, O.S. 36 watt. Pilot and number plate lamps, 6 watt. Stop/tail lamp 24/6 watt.   Ref. B/10/50.

B4

August 23, 1950.   ᵗʰᵉMotor

The Morris Minor Tourer

A Car which is Small in Size, Moderate in Performance but Outstanding for Economy and Charm

to us for test, but the most prominent of these were so quickly silenced, by a few moments' work with a screwdriver on such items as a loose horn button and a mal-adjusted door catch, that the remainder, we feel confident, were caused by equally trivial details.

It is interesting to note that, despite the need for certain reinforcement of the underframe to replace the bracing effect of the steel roof, the tourer is appreciably lighter than the saloon. It will also be noted that it nevertheless shows a slightly lower absolute maximum speed, an effect which was expected in view of the impracticability of giving a folding hood contours as smooth as those of a streamlined steel roof panel.

The bulk of our experience of the Morris Minor Tourer was gained running with the hood folded away into its neat envelope and the rear sidescreens put in their bag inside the spare wheel compartment. Run thus, it is a delightful open car,

STAGES OF OPENING.—Fully opened to the sunshine and fresh air, the Minor displays its good turning circle, while the second photograph shows that erection of the rear sidescreens increases protection against side winds without spoiling the handsome lines of the touring body.

ASSESSED upon a basis of pleasure per £, the Morris Minor tourer must be one of the best bargains available amongst present-day cars. It is not merely an open car, in itself an extremely pleasant possession, at a price below that of any other British open tourer : it also shares with the corresponding saloon that subtle charm which can make a good small car such a delightful thing to drive.

It is now 18 months since we published a Road Test Report on the Morris Minor saloon. During the intervening period we have been able to gain continuous experience of the model's ability to cope with hard and varied usage, and at the same time increasing numbers of owners all over the world have come to understand our enthusiasm for this very unusual small car.

Inevitably, in testing the touring version of this car, comparisons are made with the saloon model upon which initial production was concentrated. The cars have individual attractions which will appeal to different groups of motorists, but it can safely be said that each is fully worthy of the other.

The saloon being a car of integral steel construction, a query naturally arises as to

whether evolution of an open model, unbraced by any steel roof structure, has introduced any snags : so far as can be judged from normal driving of both models, the answer is a clear negative, roadworthiness being in no way reduced by open bodywork. There were certain rattles evident in the tourer as delivered

LENGTH AND BREADTH.—Ample footroom for rear seat passengers is provided under the tubular frames of the adjustable driving and fixed passenger seats. There is also a very ample amount of width to allow four people to remain comfortable during long journeys.

not unduly troubled by the back-draught inevitable behind a large windscreen, and with wind-down glass windows and hinged ventilation panels on the doors allowing some adjustment of the amount of fresh air blowing through the car.

With the hood raised, the car becomes closely equivalent to the saloon in internal

The Morris Minor Tourer - - - - - - - - - - - - Contd.

accommodation, weatherproofness and outward visibility. Entry to the back seats of a two-door body is never of the easiest, but the car is a very genuine and comfortable four-seater, giving very ample footroom and an amount of elbow width which eliminates any impression of smallness.

The sole disappointing feature of the touring body, in our view, is the fact that either raising or lowering the roof is a rather slow operation best carried out by two people. It may be tackled single-handed, and familiarity would expedite it, but we feel that in 1950 it should be possible to evolve a folding top which would be easier to operate without adding unduly to the cost.

A detail which is appreciated is the provision of locks on the doors, for use when the car is closed, and on the capacious luggage boot, which provides useful safe stowage for coats and gloves when the car is open.

Inside the body, there is a roomy glove box on the facia panel, and below the instruments a wide shelf with a retaining lip from which maps or papers do not blow away.

Exceptional Roadworthiness

On the road, the Morris Minor is outstanding as being one of the fastest slow cars in existence. Neither speed nor acceleration are exceptional, and in top gear the acceleration is frankly leisurely. There is however a simple four-speed gearbox which facilitates the instant use of all available engine power whenever need arises : more important, there is the sort of exceptional roadworthiness which results in maintenance of high speeds around bends and confident negotiation of small openings in traffic, the car being surprisingly seldom checked from its cruising gait.

This cruising gait is, in relation to the maximum speed of the car, unusually high, a genuine 50 m.p.h. in comparative silence as a matter of course, and 55 m.p.h. or more without protest when required. At such speeds the car rides with exceptional steadiness, the torsion bar front and leaf rear springs being extremely well damped, and holds steadily on its course while being instantly willing to alter course in response to the unusually light and sensitive steering.

Although having this delightful firmness, which makes it untiring on long day journeys, the springing system is in fact well able to absorb the shocks of potholed gravel tracks. It allows a modest amount of rolling and tyre howl to occur during fast cornering, but would be rated as excellent in all-round performance on a car of any size.

High Speeds on Third Gear

The 919 c.c. side-valve engine is extremely docile, and will happily, if not rapidly, accelerate the car from 10 m.p.h. in top gear if required. Rather unusually, it pinked on low-grade British petrol only when running at more than about 3,000 r.p.m., becoming quite prominently audible if revved hard in the indirect gears whereas in direct drive it is little heard above the small amount of wind noise which the car makes.

Incidentally, although 30 m.p.h. is perhaps the natural speed at which to change up from third into top gear, delaying the change until 40 m.p.h. greatly improves acceleration and even a further 10 m.p.h. postponement of the change is permissible occasionally.

So pleasant to drive is the Minor, thanks to its steadiness and controllability, that a tester is tempted to forget that economy of running is its essential *raison d'étre*. The fact is realised eventually, however, that although long day runs are being undertaken and the fuel tank capacity is only 5 gallons, visits to petrol filling stations are quite rare occasions. In fact, even pushing along with such vigour as Bank Holiday traffic streams across the New Forest district allowed, over 40 m.p.g. was recorded, and no abnormal restraint over cruising speed or use of the gears for acceleration is needed to produce an out-of-town fuel consumption of 50 m.p.g. As regards engine oil, 700 fast-driven miles did not lower the sump level far enough to leave room for an added pint, or incidentally produce any indication of stiffening of the easily-lubricated steering swivels.

Easy Starting

Tuned as it was for reasonable economy, the Minor's engine nevertheless started instantly after summer nights spent in the open air, and was almost immediately ready to run without use of the rich mixture control. The car carried lights adequate to its performance, although it must be admitted that on undulating roads the raised-mounting headlamps supplied to certain export markets would probably have justified their less neat appearance. Traffic indicators are fitted to the open body, but we would prefer their rather out-of-sight control to take over from the switch operating a single windscreen wiper the prominent position it occupies above the centre of the facia panel. We would also like control pedals spaced out more widely to accommodate broad country footwear, but perhaps this is impracticable with roominess obtained by extension of the body space forwards between the front wheels.

Perfection, obviously, cannot be expected of a car built to strict limits of price and size. What the Morris Minor tourer offers is practical merit in full measure, plus a very large quantity of that indefinable quality, charm.

CAPACIOUSNESS.—(Below) The large roll containing tools and wheel-changing equipment, the spare wheel, and an envelope accommodating the rear sidescreens, may be stowed in a compartment below the luggage locker. This latter is of very substantial capacity, and is provided with a lock, an appreciated detail by no means universal on open cars.

ACCESSIBILITY.—The broad bonnet, illuminated internally at night by the parking lamp bulbs, provides good access to the side-valve engine, and all auxiliaries are arranged in a spacious and correspondingly convenient manner.

The Motor Road Test No. 9/51

Make: Morris.   **Type:** Minor Four-door Saloon.
Makers: Morris Motors, Ltd., Cowley, Oxford.

Dimensions and Seating

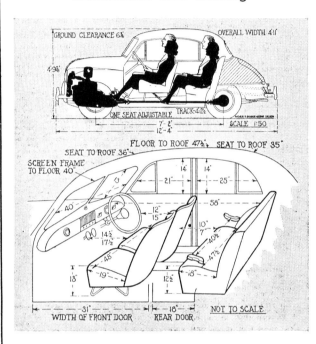

In Brief

Price, with water pump and heater, £375 10s. plus purchase tax £210 2s. 3d. equals £585 12s. 3d.

Capacity	918.6 c.c.
Unladen kerb weight	16 cwt.
Fuel consumption	39.8 m.p.g.
Maximum speed	60.1 m.p.h.
Maximum speed on 1 in 20 gradient	34 m.p.h.
Maximum top gear gradient	1 in 18

Acceleration
10-30 m.p.h. in top .. 19.9 secs.
0-50 m.p.h. through gears 37.1 secs.

Gearing 14.9 m.p.h. in top at 1,000 r.p.m., 63 m.p.h. at 2,500 ft. per min. piston speed.

Specification

Engine
Cylinders	4
Bore	57 mm.
Stroke	90 mm.
Cubic capacity	918.6 c.c.
Piston area	15.8 sq. in.
Valves	Side
Compression ratio	6.6/1
Max. power	27 b.h.p.
at	4,400 r.p.m.
Piston speed at max. b.h.p.	2,600 t. per min.
Carburetter	S.U. horizontal
Ignition	Lucas coil
Sparking plugs	14 mm, Champion L 10
Fuel pump	S.U. electric
Oil filter	Micronic

Transmission
Clutch	Borg and Beck s.d.p.
Top gear (s/m)	4.55
3rd gear (s/m)	7.015
2nd gear (s/m)	10.477
1st gear	17.944
Propeller shaft	Hardy Spicer open
Final drive	9/41 Hypoid bevel

Chassis
Brakes	Lockheed hydraulic (2 l.s.front)
Brake drum diameter	7 ins.
Friction lining area	67.2 sq. in.
Suspension: Front. Torsion bar and wishbone i.f.s.	
Rear. Semi-elliptic leaf springs	
Shock absorbers:	Armstrong hydraulic
Tyres	Dunlop 5.00 x 14

Steering
Steering gear	Rack and pinion
Turning circle	31 feet
Turns of steering wheel lock to lock	2¾

Performance factors (at laden weight as tested)
Piston area, sq. in. per ton	16.25
Brake lining area, sq. in. per ton	69.2
Specific displacement, litres per ton mile	1,900

Fully described in "The Motor," Oct. 27, 1948, Oct. 18, 1950.

Maintenance

Fuel tank: 5 gallons. **Sump:** 6½ pints, S.A.E. 30. **Gearbox and differential:** 1½ pints, S.A.E. 90 gear oil. **Rear axle:** 1½ pints, S.A.E. 90 E.P. gear oil. **Steering gear:** S.A.E. 90 gear oil. **Radiator:** 13¼ pints (1 drain tap). **Chassis lubrication:** By grease gun every 500 miles to 9 points. **Ignition timing:** T.D.C. Static. **Spark plug gap:** 0.018-0.022 in. **Contact breaker gap:** 0.012 in. **Valve timing:** Inlet opens 8 deg. before T.D.C. closes 52 deg. after B.D.C. Exhaust opens 52 deg. before B.D.C. closes 20 deg. after T.D.C. **Tappet Clearances (hot):** Inlet 0.017 in. Exhaust 0.017 in. **Front wheel toe-in:** 3/32 in. **Camber angle:** Nil. **Castor angle:** 3 deg. **Tyre pressures:** Front 22 lb., rear 22/24 lb. **Brake fluid:** Lockheed Orange (Overseas Lockheed No. 5). **Battery:** 12-volt. 38 amp/hr. **Lamp bulbs:** Head lamps, N.S. 36/36 watt, O.S. 36 watt. Pilot and number plate lamps 6 watt. Stop/tail lamp 24/6 watt. Ref. B/09/51.

Test Conditions

Showery weather, head and tail wind, smooth tarmac surface, Pool petrol.

Test Data

ACCELERATION TIMES on Two Upper Ratios

	Top	3rd
10-30 m.p.h.	19.9 secs.	10.6 secs.
20-40 m.p.h.	21.6 secs.	14.4 secs.
30-50 m.p.h.	31.6 secs.	—

ACCELERATION TIMES Through Gears

0-30 m.p.h.	10.0 secs.
0-40 m.p.h.	17.25 secs.
0-50 m.p.h.	37.1 secs.
Standing Quarter Mile	27.6 secs.

MAXIMUM SPEEDS

Flying Quarter Mile
Mean of four opposite runs	60.1 m.p.h.
Best time equals	62.6 m.p.h.

Speed in Gears
Max. speed in 3rd gear	50 m.p.h.
Max. speed in 2nd gear	37 m.p.h.
Max. speed in 1st gear	24 m.p.h.

WEIGHT

Unladen kerb weight	16 cwt.
Front/rear weight distribution	55/45
Weight laden as tested	19.5 cwt.

INSTRUMENTS

Speedometer at 30 m.p.h.	10% fast
Speedometer at 60 m.p.h.	10% fast

FUEL CONSUMPTION

52.5 m.p.g. at constant 20 m.p.h.
48.2 m.p.g. at constant 30 m.p.h.
47.3 m.p.g. at constant 40 m.p.h.
40.0 m.p.g. at constant 50 m.p.h.
Overall consumption for 385 miles,
9.7 gallons=39.8 m.p.g.

HILL CLIMBING (at steady speeds)

Max. top gear speed on 1 in 20	34 m.p.h.
Max. gradient on top gear	1 in 18 (Tapley 125 lb./ton)
Max. gradient on 3rd gear	1 in 11.2 (Tapley 200 lb./ton)
Max. gradient on 2nd gear	1 in 7.6 (Tapley 297 lb./ton)

BRAKES at 30 m.p.h.

0.91 g retardation (=33 ft. stopping distance) with 80 lb. pedal pressure
0.72 g retardation (=47 ft. stopping distance) with 50 lb. pedal pressure
0.5 g retardation (=60 ft. stopping distance) with 25 lb. pedal pressure

B16

June 20, 1951.

The Motor

The Morris Minor 4-door Saloon

A Test of the Latest Export Version of an Established Model which Shows Marked Advance in Comfort and Convenience

marked advance in the sales appeal of this type.

Conjointly with this greatly added convenience, the car has noticeably matured in respect of the internal appointments. All the established conveniences such as the full width tray under the scuttle, the inbuilt radio grille, the light that indicates where the ignition key should be inserted, the accessible centre handbrake, and the large glove locker, remain. To them are added two ashtrays, recessed into the doors on each side of the front compart-

ROAD tests of entirely new models offer an obvious and exceptional interest both for readers and for testers. If the specification is in any way unorthodox there is the question as to whether a breakaway from convention would be justified; if the design is wholly traditional it yet often occurs that the result on the road is considerably better than one might expect. When, by contrast, one is dealing with the latest manifestation of an already well-established type the possibilities of surprise are greatly reduced, and in the case of the Morris Minor Four-door Saloon which recently passed through our hands, the only change in the mechanical specification has been limited to the substitution of pump-cooling for thermo-syphon. Although this will probably prevent any loss of water in extreme mountain climbing conditions and lengthen the period between valve regrinds under conditions of full throttle operation, its principal immediate benefit has been the indirect

REFORMED—With the newly positioned head-lamps the four-door Morris Minor presents a noticeably different frontal aspect to its predecessors and retains previous excellent qualities with added features of value to the family motorist.

ROOM TO MOVE—The exceptionally wide bonnet opening discloses ample space around the simple side-valve engine and, as shown here, any accessory, including dampers, likely to need attention can readily be examined or replaced if necessary.

SPACE BEHIND—By making use of the open front seat framework, the back seat passengers on the Morris Minor are given adequate leg room despite the very modest wheelbase.

one of permitting the use of an internal heater.

Modern light cars constructed from thin gauge sheet and with a body floor that forms part of the structure and which have, in addition, the engine placed well forward and complete sealing against the entry of fumes, are by these very facts unable to offer the occupants any large measure of thermal protection and can therefore become intolerably cold in winter conditions as severe as are met with in many parts of the world. The fact that the Morris Minor can now be fitted with an interior heater is therefore not so small a detail as might be supposed, but a matter of prime importance for overseas buyers (to whom the sale of this type is at present restricted) who might otherwise deny themselves the economy, convenience and pleasure to be had in driving this exemplary small car.

There can further be no doubt that for family motoring four doors are an even greater convenience on a small car than on larger models, and thus the introduction of a Minor at the end of last year with two doors on each side represents another

ment, and a third in the centre of the propeller shaft tunnel at the back, straps to assist shutting the doors, and greatly improved door locks and handles, whilst a roof-light is an additional feature which is well worth its place. There is also ample indication that draught-proofing has been the subject of special study, although the car submitted for test could not be passed as 100 per cent. satisfactory in this respect.

Comparative Performance

As compared with the two-door saloon tested as far back as February 1949, the weight has increased by five per cent and on cars with rather low displacement factors even such a very small change can have a marked effect on the overall performance. It is therefore not surprising that the maximum gradient climbable in top gear has fallen to 1 in 18 as compared with 1 in 16 on the previous two-door saloon, and that the standing ¼-mile time has been raised from 26.3 to 27.6 seconds. With a maximum speed of fractionally over 60 m.p.h. the later car was also somewhat the slower of the two,

FEATURES OF VALUE—The luggage locker of the Morris Minor is entirely separate from the spare wheel housing and is of ample size. The engine can now be supplied with a water pump which permits the installation of an effective heater and de-mister beneath the facia panel as shown immediately above.

The Morris Minor 4-door Saloon - - - - - - - Contd.

but any change in this respect may be considered as within the limits of error as between one particular car and another tested on different days. More important to the type of motorist who is likely to buy this kind of car, the fuel consumption has remained almost unchanged, and the figure given of fractionally under 40 m.p.g. is based upon considerably harder driving than would be employed by the majority of owners.

It must, however, be admitted that the four-door Minor, like both its two-door predecessor and the Tourer, is a car which encourages brisk driving methods. High gearing, which brings the road speed at 2,500 ft.-min. piston speed to virtually an equality with the maximum speed, makes it possible to run at 50 to 60 m.p.h. on the open road with little or no sign of effort from the engine. But by reason of the modest acceleration from low speeds on top gear, there is every incentive to make free use of the quiet gear box which has such an admirably easy gear change that the change-down into third at, say, 40 m.p.h. or into second at 25 m.p.h. quickly becomes automatic—and can indeed be silently effected without touching the clutch if the driver has a reasonably good ear. This method of driving does, however, imply that the engine is frequently running between 3,500 and 4,500 r.p.m. and to some extent, impair the overall fuel consumption.

Exceptional Road Holding

In some ways the quite exceptional road holding and cornering power of the car work towards the same end. Normal small cars often have their road speed reduced either by poor surfaces or a sinuous route but the torsion bar independent front suspension, the ample damping, and carefully contrived weight distribution of the Minor give a remarkable ride over rough roads, whilst the light, sensitive, high geared, rack and pinion steering, relatively wide track, and low centre of gravity provide cornering powers which are rivalled only by a few Continental sports cars. As a consequence of these attributes the overall average speed abilities of the Morris Minor are almost absurdly disproportionate to the performance on paper and it is possible easily to cover 120 miles in less than three

hours with two up, or in very little more than this time fully laden.

From a strictly utilitarian point of view one may therefore say that the new Morris Minor four-door Saloon is well equipped, represents a definite advance in convenience and combines potentially high average speeds with a very limited appetite for fuel. Over and above the utilitarian aspect, it is a car which must appeal very largely to anyone who enjoys driving for driving's sake, for it reproduces, albeit within a limited frame of reference, all the best concepts of modern practice in handling and road worthiness.

It must be admitted that to the vast majority of potential buyers, particularly those overseas, these features which appeal to the expert driver may seem like "the glories of our blood and race," but "shadows, not substantial things." They will be more concerned with such humdrum aspects as interior accommodation, luggage space and ease of servicing.

Four in Comfort

As can be seen from the diagram, the width of the Minor body shell is such that four people can be accommodated with the greatest ease, and the carriage of three adults on the rear seats is by no means impossible. Back seat passengers have but limited leg room but the open framework of the individual front seats makes it possible for them easily to place their feet below the front seat cushions, and as can be seen from an illustration there need be no question of cramp for a person of average size. The addition of armrests on the doors also materially increases the comfort of the back compartment whilst the windows both in their depth and arrangement are such as to provide a very good sideways and forwards outlook. The rear luggage locker also has a large cubic content and it should be noted that with two up the back of the rear seat can be swung forward. It is then possible to carry exceptionally large objects supported partly in the luggage locker and partly in the body itself. It will be seen from the side elevation of the car that the pedals are mounted slightly forward of the wheel arch—a process which gives exceptional leg room on a limited wheel base at the cost of having the pedals rather close together—a fact which may cause

some initial confusion which soon disappears. Forward visibility straight ahead over the falling bonnet is good, but the rather thick front pillar, triangulated ventilation window and centre strip for the vee screen, combine to obstruct somewhat the sideways view, and this disability is felt increasingly as the adjustable driver's seat is moved back on its traverse. Generally speaking, however, the passenger space available is far greater than one would suppose from viewing the exterior of the car and long journeys can be made in comfort with three or four persons aboard.

Real Access

The accessibility of the engine is also worthy of praise. The bonnet opens almost to the width of the track and the electric fuel pump, carburetter, ignition, components and dynamo can all readily be reached for adjustment or replacement if necessary. The accessibility of the tappets on a side valve engine of this kind presents inherent problems, but the operation does not on this model cause serious difficulties.

It will be observed from the illustrations that the headlamps are now raised and submerged within the wings, and although this gives a changed outline it does not appear materially to have affected the road illumination, and on the car supplied for test (which retained the now obsolescent dip and switch system) the short range in the dip condition might well be considered dangerous. One must also condemn the horn as having inadequate power, whilst the press and welding work immediately above the parcel tray was well designed to draw blood from any hand which might happen to make contact with it. The central gear lever may also be thought rather too short if the driver's seat is put in the furthest back position. In these circumstances, also, the direction indicator switch (which is now self-cancelling) is not particularly easy to reach, and in any case demands that the driver's right hand be removed from the wheel for some appreciable time.

The interior heater which has been mentioned is of the re-circulating type with a feed to the back of the windscreen and, although mechanically noisy, seemed, within the limits of a test in moderate weather, to have ample thermal capacity.

Super Profile

Side-valve to Overhead Valve

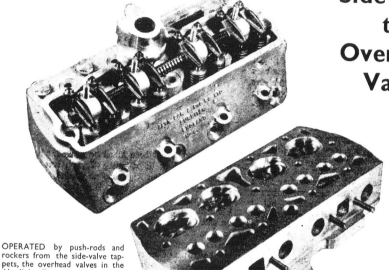

OPERATED by push-rods and rockers from the side-valve tappets, the overhead valves in the Alta light-alloy cylinder head are set in a line, sparking plugs adjoining the exhaust valves. Porting has been arranged so that the existing manifolds may be used, consequently twin-carburetter installations designed for the side-valve engine remain applicable to the overhead-valve conversion.

in second gear and on to a genuine 50 m.p.h. in third gear, the car very easily reaches the 60-65 m.p.h. at which it seems happy to cruise. Accelerating either from rest through the gears or from 10 m.p.h. in top gear only, the car with the o.h.v. conversion reaches 65 m.p.h. in the time which a s.v. model would take to reach 50 m.p.h.

Interestingly, fuel consumption seems to be little affected by the conversion to o.h.v., actually showing an improvement at low speeds and only dropping to 30 m.p.g. in very fast driving. It is unfortunate that the car for which this conversion is designed has now given place to a lower-geared model with a smaller engine, but the possibility of obtaining over 70 m.p.h. may

A Test of the Alta Conversion for the Morris Minor Series MM

NOW superseded by the Series II car with 803 c.c. o.h.v. engine, the 918 c.c. Series MM Morris Minor always tantalized keen drivers. It had beautiful handling qualities, a rear axle ratio high enough for fast cruising, a delightful four-speed gearbox, but very little power. We have recently been able to sample one of these cars which has been quite transformed in character by the fitting of an overhead-valve cylinder head produced by the manufacturers of Alta racing cars.

Sold by the Alta Car and Engineering Co., Ltd., Fullers Way, Kingston By-pass, Surrey, for £45 complete with all gaskets and other parts needed for fitting (this work can be done by the makers for £4 if required), the new

cylinder head is illustrated on this page. Cast in aluminium, it carries a single line of inclined overhead valves, with dual springs, which are operated by push-rods and forged rockers from the tappets of the original side-valve engine. Inserted Brico valve seatings are used, and the inlet valve diameter is increased by 2 mm. Designed to give a compression ratio of 8¼ : 1 which requires (and makes good use of) present-day high-octane fuel, this cylinder head is designed with siamesed inlet ports, so that the usual Morris inlet and exhaust manifolds bolt straight onto it, the only changes being a short exhaust pipe extension and a different jet needle in the S.U. carburetter.

Our tests were made on a very well-worn car with an appreciable thirst for oil, a car which has been raced quite frequently and which had a Servais silencer (not causing undue amounts of exhaust noise) and was running without a fan. As the comparative figures show, the customary gentle top-gear acceleration of the Minor from low speeds is usefully improved. The real gain, however, is in power at high r.p.m., as indicated by the graph computed from our road test figures. Maximum speed in top gear goes up from around 60 m.p.h. to over 73 m.p.h., a pace sufficient to carry the optimistic speedometer right off its scale. With really useful acceleration up to over 30 m.p.h.

tempt quite a number of people to keep examples of the Series MM Morris Minor in commission.

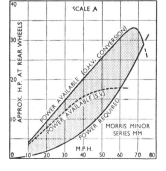

OWNER'S VIEW

Ray Newell interviews Roger Horton, owner of a very desirable 1950 Morris Minor 'lowlight' M.M. Tourer, RVW 178. Roger is a classic car enthusiast of some years' standing who lists amongst his previous cars a 4-litre Vanden Plas Princess and an Aston Martin DB 2/4 Tickford-bodied special. Roger and his wife live in Hunsden, near Ware, Hertfordshire.

R.N. When did you first become interested in Morris Minors?
R.H. In 1971 when I bought my Series M.M. Tourer for £90.
R.N. What prompted you to buy this particular car?
R.H. I was looking for a car to tide me over for a short time. I had just sold my Vanden Plas Princess and RVW 178 was intended to be a stopgap car.
R.N. Obviously it has become something more than that. What changed your mind?
R.H. Well it was a sound car and it turned out to be very reliable. I decided to use it for everyday transport. Mind you it did seem a bit slow after a 4000cc Princess.
R.N. What sort of condition was the car in at this time?
R.H. It was a sound enough car but it looked dull and scruffy. It had been painted dark blue and it had a dark red hood which leaked at all corners.

R.N. I understand that you entered the car in an unusual competition soon after this.
R.H. Yes, the Sunday People newspaper was running a national competition for 'old bangers' and home-decorated cars. By this time I had treated 'Morris' to a new white hood and two coats of light blue Dulux (hand painted of course!). I entered 'Morris' in the 'old bangers' class and from thousands of entrants it was picked as one of the twenty vehicles to attend the finals at Woburn Abbey in January 1973. 'Morris' didn't win but was highly commended. Rally Driver Roger Clark who presented the awards couldn't believe Morris was hand painted, the finish was so good.
R.N. At what stage did you undertake the major restoration which has brought the car to its present pristine condition?
R.H. In November 1976 the engine began losing power due to a split exhaust valve. I decided to take the car off the road. It stayed in the garage until May 1978 when I began a full scale rebuild.
R.N. What precisely did the restoration involve?
R.H. First of all the car was completely dismantled. Every part was catalogued and stored in numbered tea chests, the condition of every part was noted and a list of new parts needed was compiled. This list eventually exceeded 150 parts not counting new nuts, bolts and washers. The bodyshell was completely stripped of paint inside and out, down to bare metal. The underside of the floor and the chassis sections were very thoroughly inspected; all the rust damage and weak spots were noted on a carefully prepared plan and submitted to a professional welder who had agreed to undertake the job. After the welding had been done the process of rebuilding commenced. This took four years of slow, painstaking work. Wherever possible, parts were reconditioned rather than replaced so as to keep items such as the engine gearbox, rear axle,

starter, dynamo and all auxiliary parts original. The interior was completely re-upholstered and new carpets were fitted. After some initial problems over getting a new hood made, the job was finally completed in 1982.
R.N. In the light of your experience, what advice would you offer to other M.M. owners tackling a major restoration?
R.H. Two things. First make a catalogue of all parts removed from the car. This can save hours when the process of rebuilding takes place months or years later. Second, pay particular attention to rust-damaged areas and have them repaired properly. In my opinion this is the most important stage of any restoration. Any inferior workmanship or corner cutting at this stage renders all future work a complete waste of time and money.
R.N. In the course of your restoration did you encounter any difficulties obtaining parts? You mentioned earlier you made a list of 150 new parts needed.
R.H. Yes, I most certainly did. I was unable to obtain many new body parts including front wings, bumper blades and valances, a front panel and a bonnet. On the mechanical side I had difficulty getting front wheel cylinders and I couldn't get any swivel pins or front brake drum hubs.
R.N. In your quest for parts did you find any specialist firms particularly useful?
R.H. Yes, two firms in particular were very helpful in retrimming the car. Edgware Motor Accessories recovered the seats and provided the body trimmings and The Don Trimming Co. Ltd made the hood.
R.N. Are you a member of a Car Club for Series M.M. Morris Minors?
R.H. Yes, I'm a member of the Morris Minor Owners Club.
R.N. What do you find most valuable about this club?
R.H. I find the Morris Minor Owners Club very useful. The rallies which I attend quite frequently, are always well organised. I find it interesting

to see how other members have restored their cars and I like to compare the methods they have used and their priorities in attention to detail and originality.

R.N. With a car like yours you must have entered numerous Concours competitions. How successful have you been?

R.H. Quite successful. My car attained Masters Status at the M.M.O.C. National Rally in 1982 and has retained that ever since. I have won quite a few awards and have represented the club at the Brighton Classic Car Show.

R.N. How would you sum up the pleasure you get from owning and driving your Series M.M. Tourer?

R.H. In my opinion the Series M.M. was the last true Morris to leave Cowley. I think it's always an attraction to have one of the oldest or the rarest or the most desirable models of any one-make car club. The Series M.M. lowlight Tourer fits the bill for me in this respect. However, as far as driving is concerned, the M.M. is not really up to today's motoring standards. In town it tends to be slow away from lights, and on the open road I rarely exceed 50mph. The road holding is still very good, and for a thirty-four year old car it looks quite modern. It most definitely is not a car to be used for a high yearly mileage particularly as spares become increasingly hard to find – unlike its successor, the Morris 1000.

R.N. Finally, Roger, I know that you have spent a lot of money restoring your car to its present condition. In fact you could have bought a new Mini with the money you've spent. What advice would you give to someone buying a Series M.M. car.

R.H. Take your time in selecting the car you want to buy. Unless you can do most of the restoration work yourself choose a vehicle in the best possible condition – allowing for its age of course. Take someone with you who knows the Series M.M. cars well if you are uncertain about your purchase and if you are buying an early type Series M.M. be prepared to put up with some

frustration because new spare parts are not readily available.

Ray Newell interviews Bob Terry, an Australian Morris Minor enthusiast and owner of three Series M.M. cars. Bob is a member of the Morris Minor Car Club of Victoria and part of the organising committee for the 2nd Australian National Rally.

R.N. When did you first become interested in Morris Minors?

B.T. Approximately five years ago. While out travelling I spotted a grey 'lowlight' sedan buried up to its axle in mud. I brought it for $35 but it was eighteen months before I started any restoration work.

R.N. How many Morris Minors have you owned?

B.T. In the last five years I have owned three Morris 1000s, one 4 door Series II sedan, two 'lowlight' Series M.M. sedans and one Series M.M. Tourer.

R.N. Which of the models do you prefer?

B.T. I much prefer the Series M.M. lowlight models.

R.N. Why do you favour the Series M.M. models?

B.T. I prefer their simplistic general design and I find that they are extremely reliable and relatively comfortable. They have lasting appeal and to use the words of Winston Churchill, "they were the first beginnings, modest, tentative but insinuating."

R.N. What sort of condition were the cars in when you bought them?

B.T. Other than the lowlight convertible and the sedan which we are now using, all the vehicles were structurally very sound. An occasional valve grind, gearbox overhaul or general bush replacement seem the most common requirements. The vehicles that I have selected, have in the main been somewhat dirty and neglected but they clean up very well.

R.N. What repairs have you carried out on the vehicles?

B.T. The lowlight tourer has been a major restoration project and I shall be very pleased to see it finished. It comprises two vehicles, the front end of the original tourer and the rear end from a high light M.M. sedan. A lot of work was involved in getting the car to look like something worthwhile. Mechanical restoration is nearly complete and the final assembly of the engine is now under way. The paintwork I intend to do myself, within the next two months.

R.N. Do you regard your vehicles as having been 'good buys' when you look back at the money you have spent restoring them?

B.T. In the case of the 1950 sedan I have spent very little – certainly compared to the 1948 Tourer it was a good buy. In the case of the tourer you have to balance expenditure against the fact that it is a rare car. I would estimate that there are no more than twenty registered in the state of Victoria. Having said this I still have to face the fact that it has been an expensive car to restore but I'm confident the finished product will make it all worthwhile.

R.N. How readily available are spare parts for the M.M.s in Australia?

B.T. New parts are a little difficult to obtain. Rubber parts are good. Engine parts such as valves, springs and guides are nearly impossible. Front wheel cylinders and some gearbox parts are a no-no. Bodywise, diecast (chrome) components such as hockey sticks, door catch plates etc., are a definite no. Secondhand parts are generally available but their condition is never very good. As club members get together and inter-state contacts develop, the situation should improve.

R.N. Who are the main specialist firms who provide spares for these vehicles in Australia?

B.T. There are two main companies – The Morris Minor Centre of Australia and the Morris Minor Company of Australia.

R.N. What method of obtaining spares do you find most useful?

B.T. My major source of supply is the club swap meetings, but as you might imagine not too much swapping goes on.

R.N. How much contact do you have with M.M. owners in the U.K.?

B.T. Other than yourself, none. But I would be pleased to correspond.

B.T. How practical is the M.M. for use in Australia in the 1980s?

B.T. Economy-wise it is a real winner but in today's traffic it can be something of a liability. The lack of V8 power in a hilly terrain can make driving a little unnerving but – what's the hurry? I delight in it.

R.N. Have you had any modifications fitted to your car to improve its performance?

B.T. Yes, our original intention was to use the vehicle as much as possible as a local runabout. It is modified slightly without upsetting the general appearance too much. A Monaro twin carburettor set was fitted and the exhaust system increased to $1\frac{1}{4}$ in O.D. from the larger silencer. Flashing indicators were fitted in preference to the trafficators.

R.N. What value do you get from the Owners Club to which you belong?

B.T. I find the magazine of the British club very informative and interesting.

R.N. What co-operation exists between the Australian Morris Minor Owners Clubs?

B.T. There are many active groups in Victoria with close unity with the Melbourne-based club.

R.N. Are there any special

advantages for owners of Series M.M. cars in the clubs?

B.T. No. Overall there are approximately 7-8 members who own Series M.M. cars. Within the Morris Register of fifty members only about four would have these vehicles.

R.N. Australia was the top export market for the Series M.M. vehicle. Thirty years on how possible would it be to find a good lowlight tourer to import back into Britain?

B.T. The tourer is very popular with the young people and they command high prices. I do not know of any. The day does not go by without a tourer being featured in a T.V. commercial. Several sedans have been converted into tourers. They are fitted with Datsun 1200 engines and auto transmissions in some cases. The structural strength of the side rails is dubious after all these years. The police are becoming aware of this rehash situation and are taking action.

Ray Newell interviews Peter Gamble, the owner of the highly acclaimed 1952 Series M.M. Saloon, MRW 797, winner of the National Classic Car Concours in 1980, the Post-War Classic Car Award at the 1982 Northern Classic Car Show and numerous other club awards and trophies. Peter lives in Derby with his wife Pat and three children.

R.N. When did you first become interested in Morris Minors?

P.G. In 1965 when I bought a new Traveller. However, my interest at this time was shortlived as it was quite troublesome and I sold it nine months later.

R.N. When did you acquire the Morris Minors you own now?

P.G. I bought my Series M.M. Saloon in 1974, the family 1000 Traveller in 1978 and a 1953 M.M. Tourer for my son, John, in 1979. The tourer incidentally is still undergoing an extensive restoration.

R.N. What was the condition of

your M.M. saloon when you bought it?

P.G. Structurally it was very sound. The bodywork was in good condition but mechanically it was in need of immediate attention – particularly the engine.

R.N. What repairs/renovations have you carried out on the car?

P.G. Initially, my aim was to make the car a reliable means of transport. My first priority was to rebuild the engine totally. This done, I turned my attention to the gearbox which was also faulty. I decided to install a replacement gearbox at that stage in order to make it a viable means of transport. I still have the original gearbox and I hope at some stage to overhaul and refit it. I then used the car as everyday transport for about three years during which time I encountered no major problems. Towards the end of 1977 I began what has become an ongoing process of refurbishing the entire vehicle. I've done this in stages taking great care over every job and indeed I'm still looking for ways of improving its condition.

R.N. That must be difficult, Peter, it seems immaculate in all aspects.

P.G. Almost all aspects.

R.N. Looking back, do you think you would have been any better off buying a car in better condition than yours initially?

P.G. No, not really. It was basically sound and it served me well as everyday transport in the first instance.

R.N. Have you had any difficulties in obtaining spare parts for your M.M?

P.G. Yes. In 1974 it was very difficult, but with my involvement in the Morris Minor Owners Club as M.M. Spares Secretary I became much more aware of the potential of 'autojumble' and began an intensive period of tracing and selling M.M. spares for the Club. Consequently I have become quite conversant with the spares scene and over the years I've built up my own personal stock. I've never really been stuck for anything.

R.N. Is there a particular Morris Minor specialist you have found useful?

P.G. Yes, Henric in Nottingham are particularly good for body panels. However there is no-one who just specialises in M.M. spares, which is a pity.

R.N. How practical is your M.M. for everyday use?

P.G. It's adequately practical even with three children as passengers. Economy is good and service spares are easily available.

R.N. How would you sum up the enjoyment you get from owning and driving your M.M?

P.G. I get great pleasure from driving it because of its present condition – considering its age. In its own way it's as different as owning a Rolls-Royce. It's a car which people can associate with; it's a social leveller. I've made a lot of friends through owning this particular car and through my involvement in the Morris Minor Owners Club.

R.N. What would you say are the advantages of belonging to a car club like the M.M.O.C?

P.G. I think more than anything, the opportunity to meet with people with similar motoring interests. The Clubs themselves provide a lot of useful services. The Morris Minor Owners Club in particular stages rallies all over Britain and produces a very good magazine as well as providing access for members to useful spares.

R.N. What advice would you give to someone contemplating buying a Series M.M. car?

P.G. My advice would be to read as much background information as possible about your particular choice of M.M. so that you have an idea of what to look for. I would strongly recommend taking someone along with you who knows M.M.s and whose opinion you respect.

R.N. As a successful competitor in many concours competitions over the years, what advice would you give to the would-be concours entrant just preparing his car?

P.G. In one sentence? Be as thorough as is humanly possible in every job you do.

R.N. Finally, Peter, has owning your Series M.M. car provided you with any interesting or unusual experiences?

P.G. Oh yes. When I'm out in the car I often return to the car park to find it surrounded by an 'inspection committee' who are usually most appreciative and friendly. On one occasion I found a pair of legs sticking out from under my car. As I approached, a voice from under said, "Yes, it is a side-valve", to his embarrassed wife standing next to me.

BUYING

For many people the charm and character of the Morris Minor is embodied more in the first series of cars than in any of the subsequent models. However, the purchase of a Series M.M. Morris Minor is not something to be undertaken lightly. The fact that the youngest Series M.M. car will be well over thirty years old has, in itself, serious implications for the intending purchaser. Not least of these will be the question of the availability of the various models.

Series M.M. cars are much less abundant than their successor, the Morris 1000. In all, 176,002 Series M.M.s were produced but not surprisingly the ravages of time – and rust – have taken a considerable toll on this original total. Would-be purchasers of early models in Britain face a difficult task in locating 'lowlight' M.M.s, mainly because of the historical fact that upwards of 80% of 2 door saloons and tourers were exported in the early years. Even when the 'high headlamp' Series M.M. 4 door saloon was introduced in 1950 it was available only for export in the first instance. Though the percentage of cars exported remained high, the increase in overall production in later years means that the most common surviving models found in Britain are the 2 door and 4 door saloons

manufactured from 1951 onwards.

Models prior to this are much more elusive and anyone searching for a 1948 Morris Minor Series M.M. Tourer, arguably the most desirable model to carry the name Morris Minor, faces a particularly difficult task.

The choice of other models is largely one of personal preference. The joys of open-top motoring have to be tempered with the acceptance of the fact that tourers tend to be more prone to leaks and draughts than saloons. The choice between a 2 or 4 door saloon is really a question of individual requirements and availability.

Assuming that the intending purchaser has given serious thought to the specific purchase of a Series M.M. and that he is not simply buying an old Morris Minor, it is likely that he will already have come to terms with certain facts. He will have realised that he cannot realistically expect startling performance figures due to the limitations of the side-valve engine, that driving a vehicle with restricted rear vision and semaphore indicators will present its own problems in dense, modern, traffic and that he will be the owner of a vehicle for which some spare parts will be difficult to obtain.

It may well be that he will already have subscribed to the view held by many other owners, that the Series M.M. is not ideally suited for everyday motoring in the demanding circumstances of the

1980s, that he will have already decided to compromise on originality in the interests of safety by fitting extras such as wing mirrors and flashing indicators and that he views his purchase as an investment to be cherished and perhaps used as a second car.

Regardless of the ultimate use to which the car will be put, a number of options are open to those who wish to buy a Series M.M. The most critical decision is whether to buy a car which in advertising jargon is 'ripe for restoration', 'basically sound' or 'A1 in all respects'. Whichever way is chosen, attention to the following details may prove beneficial.

Problem Areas

Bodywork

The problem areas most commonly encountered on Morris Minors, and the most serious, are those associated with bodywork. In this respect the Series M.M. is no exception, though to be fair many have survived in better condition than many of the later Minor 1000 models. This may be partly due to the rust-proofing process which was adopted at Cowley early on in the production of the Series M.M. A quarter of a million pounds was spent at the works installing a 'Rotodip' plant which ensured that all cars were completely rustproofed inside and out and had a primer coat of paint keyed on and stoved before final paint finishing took place.

Nevertheless even this preventative measure has not totally eradicated rust. The most obvious areas which are prone to rust are the external panels. Front wings rust near to the front door line and around the headlamps on the later style M.M. wings. Rear wings tend to rust around the beading close to the body. The bottom edges of rear wings, door and the boot lid are all areas where rusting occurs.

Super Profile

Less obvious, but more critical, are the structural areas on the underside of the vehicles which are prone to rusting. These include the front chassis members, the central cross member and the jacking points each side of the car, the rear springer mounting points and the floor pan itself.

The intending buyer would be well advised to check all these areas meticulously and then consider the availability of replacement or repair panels.

Early type front wings are virtually unobtainable and repair is the only realistic answer until such times as someone feels it is practical to produce a limited run. Later type original front wings are also difficult to obtain although most people fit later '1000' wings and modify them. Similarly the original 'deep cut' rear wings are becoming increasingly difficult to obtain though reshaped '1000' wings are available.

Most of the body panels on the Series M.M. are different from Morris Minor models though early Series II cars can be a useful source of supply for some later M.M. parts. Early type bonnets, doors and grille panels are different and difficult to obtain new. In the case of doors, an exchange/repair scheme is operated by some of the leading Morris Minor specialists. A similar scheme operates for the repair of boot lids.

Replacement/repair panels for the underside are less difficult to obtain although effective repairs can be time consuming and expensive. Sufficient specialists now offer restoration services to enable the prospective customer a fair degree of choice. Indeed the latest development is the production of a complete underside for a Morris Minor!

Interior and Exterior Trim
The condition of the interior of the vehicle is a point often overlooked by intending purchasers – often to their cost. For anyone buying a Series M.M. particular attention

30

should be paid to the following items. The condition of the leather seat facings should be carefully noted. Splits and tears are difficult to repair and even the stitching on worn leather can prove difficult to repair. A check should be made, too, on the condition of carpets. If originality is a priority for the buyer Karvel carpets should be fitted. However these are no longer available!

On early Series M.Ms a cloth-covered board headlining was fitted. Over thirty years on, many of these are the worse for wear, particularly on the section under the rear screen. The D.I.Y. handyman may care to undertake the task of recovering the 'boards' using a special type of glue which will not soak through cloth and a suitable cloth such as 'West of England'. An alternative 'non-original' solution is to fit a good second-hand rexine-type board lining out of a later M.M.

Attention should be paid to the front and rear screen rubbers. These are usually available from Morris Minor specialists and owners' clubs.

Chrome trim can present problems if it needs to be replaced. Certain items for the Series M.M., such as early type bonnet hinges, are virtually unobtainable and the only solution is to have them rechromed. Due to the fact that the chrome parts fitted to Morris Minors were made from the metal 'Masak' they tend to 'pit' in time.

Items are difficult to repolish and some replating firms are reluctant to undertake rechroming. Other items such as the windscreen pillar, rear boot badges and front hockey sticks have been reproduced by clubs and specialist firms and are readily available. The hinges and door handles of later M.M.s are interchangeable with Morris 1000 parts and are much more easily obtained. Items such as bumpers, blades and over-riders present no problem as far as replating is concerned.

Engine
The 918cc side-valve engine is a robust, reliable unit which is relatively easy to work on and repair. The thermosyphon cooling system can be problematic in models not fitted with a water pump. A check should be made to establish that a thermostat has not been fitted to these models as they restrict the flow too much in the thermosyphon system. Careful checks should be made on ignition settings too. Settings too far advanced or retarded cause overheating in these engines. On cars fitted with water pumps a thermostat can be used to advantage. A higher temperature setting than 72°C should not be used – 68°C is ideal. Otherwise on a long hard journey water may be lost due to local boiling in the system.

Careful attention should also be paid to the thermostat housing cover which has a tendency to corrode away causing water leaks. This also applies to the aluminium side water cover fitted to later models.

All year round use of an antifreeze compatible with aluminium is advantageous in reducing corrosion and in preventing the build-up of sludge in the cooling system.

Tappet adjustment on side-valve engines is a difficult and often neglected job. Coupled with too weak a mixture setting, this can contribute to 'burnt out' exhaust valves. Engine performance depends greatly on the correct setting of ignition timing. However this can be seriously affected by badly worn distributor brushes caused by lack of lubrication. The result is 'side shake' which results in over advancement of the ignition timing and 'knocking' when the engine is running. The worn distributor bearings should be replaced and lubricated sparingly at regular intervals.

Gearbox

The Series M.M. gearbox is a thoroughly dependable unit and few problems arise. Any problems tend to be centred around the gear lever conical spring which can make gear changing difficult and can sometimes break. Bearings for the gearbox are readily available from specialist engineering firms.

Front suspension

The main problem which is associated with the suspension of the Series M.M. is the replacement of swivel pins. These are in short supply and are not available from British Leyland suppliers. The swivel pins on the Series M.M. are unique to that model and are fundamentally different from the later Morris 1000. The size of the stub axle is the critical feature. Both are the same length but the M.M. diameter is $\frac{7}{8}$in maximum and $\frac{5}{8}$in minimum, while the Morris 1000 dimensions are 25mm and 175mm respectively.

There are various solutions to the problem. Fitting a swivel from a Minor 1000 will entail fitting the hub and wheel also. Alternatively a sleeve can be made to fit into the 1000 swivel and the M.M. stub axle can then be pressed into this. However, if this method is adopted, care must be taken to ensure that the stub axle is located axially as it could work its way out. The best solution is to machine out the M.M. hub to take 25mm and 17mm inner diameter bearings. With this method the M.M. hub and wheel can be retained and the later more easily available Minor 1000 swivel

pins assembly can be used. It is feasible to machine down the outer part of the Minor 1000 stub axle to M.M. dimensions but this is *not* recommended, as the machining gives a step in the stub axle at the point of maximum bending moment. This 'stress raiser' can cause fatigue and ultimately the failure of the stub axle with consequent loss of the road wheel, brakes and control.

Road Wheels

The design of the road wheels on the Series M.M. differs from that of later Morris Minor 1000s; they are not interchangeable. The early type wheels in comparison are much more fragile and the bolt type fittings can be troublesome. The wheels can become loose on the retaining bolts even when they are fully tight. This is caused by excessive wear on the countersink in the wheel into which the bolt fits. An easy solution is to fit a $\frac{7}{16}$in mild steel washer $\frac{1}{16}$in thick under the bolt head. Tightening the bolt will form the washer into the countersink, so taking up the wear.

Brakes

Brakes on the Series M.M. can seize 'on' or 'off', causing pulling to one side when the car is being driven. Part of the problem is in the design of the brake cylinders. The cylinders are aluminium and the pistons are steel. Corrosion occurs between the two metals causing malfunction of the brakes.

Repair is possible by thorough cleaning and polishing of the cylinder bore if corrosion is not too far advanced. Otherwise replacement with new cylinders is the only answer. The prevention of further internal corrosion in the brake system can be achieved by using silicone brake fluid – an increasingly popular product with 'classic car owners'.

Historical Value Patterns

When the Morris Minor was

introduced in 1948, 2 door saloons and tourer versions sold for the same all-inclusive price of £358 10s. 7d. In succeeding years prices increased slightly and when the 4 door saloon became available in late 1950, albeit for the export market, the all-inclusive price was £585 12s 3d.

In the early years, second-hand prices of Series M.M.s remained high. Both *Motor* and *Autocar* reviewed second-hand prices in the mid-1950s and noted that depreciation was slow. *Motor* commented thus, "the slow depreciation of the Morris Minor – to the extent that some four year old examples are still being sold on the used car market at more than the original basic price when new – is a tribute to the success and reflects its wide popularity."

Today prices for Series M.M. saloons and tourers depend as one would expect upon condition and they vary tremendously. With the possible exception of 'lowlight' tourers, which are much sought after by collectors and generally command high prices, it is very much a buyers' market. Sound reliable runners can be bought for realistic prices as can viable restoration projects; original low mileage and 'concours' vehicles command much higher prices.

Whether the intrinsic value of the first Series of Morris Minors increases in the future remains to be seen. Only time will tell.

Summing Up

Anyone wishing to buy a Morris Minor Series M.M. would be well advised to adopt a patient attitude and search through the motoring magazines which advertise 'classic cars' for sale. This is particularly true if their quest is for a 'lowlight' model.

In addition to the facts already mentioned, the purchaser would be well advised to collect together original documents and as much of the history of the vehicle as possible. This may well add to its value in a future transaction.

Membership of a recognised car club is strongly recommended as amongst other things it may well help in locating sources for spare parts. Owning an older 'classic car' is a hobby which has to be worked at. Any Series M.M. owners who expect the current interest in Morris Minors and the increase in the number of specialist firms to provide fully for his needs will be disappointed.

Nevertheless, once aware of the problems and potential difficulties of owning, running and restoring a Series M.M., they can look forward to ownership of a vehicle of character with a good investment potential.

CLUBS, SPECIALISTS & BOOKS

Owners of classic cars will readily testify to the importance of one-make car clubs, specialist firms and relevant publications in helping to keep their vehicles on the road and in aiding restoration projects. In this respect owners of Series M.M. Morris Minors are no exception.

Over thirty years have passed since the last Series M.M. was produced at Cowley. Some parts are now almost impossible to obtain and queries continually arise over specifications, paint types and colours and interior trim.

The needs and interests of the Series M.M. owner tend to be served by one-make car clubs and specialists which encompass the whole range of Morris Minors produced between 1948-71. While this is logical from the point of view of owners' clubs and understandable to some extent from an economic point of view as far as specialist firms are concerned, the fact remains that no organisation or specialist firm exists which deals exclusively with Series M.M. cars.

This section considers some of the clubs, specialists and books which the author feels may be of interest to Series M.M. owners. It should be noted that as far as specialist firms are concerned the list is only representative of particular services offered and has been compiled by the author on the basis of personal experience or recommendation. No doubt – in certain cases – other specialists exist who offer comparable services.

Clubs

Morris Minor Owners Club

This is the largest car club exclusively for owners of post-war Morris Minors. Established in 1977 this fast growing national club provides a wide ranging service for its large membership. Contact is maintained via a well-produced and informative bi-monthly magazine, *Minor Matters,* by informal monthly meetings at over forty branches throughout the United Kingdom and by branch, regional, national and international rallies and events. The club also provides for its members technical advice and access to a comprehensive spares service including some specially manufactured Series M.M. parts. Other benefits include negotiated discounts on certain spares, services and insurance. Club contact: Jane Flanders, 127-129 Green Lane, Derby, England.

Series M.M. Register

In 1983 the Morris Minor Owners Club extended its registry facility to include Series M.M. Cars. The Club's other register is for Series II Travellers. The purpose of the register is to identify and catalogue as many of the surviving Series M.M. cars as possible and to establish a point of contact between Series M.M. owners. Although organised from within the Morris Minors Owners Club the register is open to owners of M.M. cars throughout the World. Registrar: Ray Newell, 84 High Street, Loscoe, Derbyshire, DE7 7LF, England.

North East Morris Minor Club

A club with over three hundred members which welcomes Series M.M. owners. Monthly meetings are arranged and a newsletter is circulated to members once a month too. This club actively supports local rallies and events and provides a useful spares service for its members.
Club contact: Samantha Davey, 91 Hatfield Place, Peterlee, Co. Durham, England.

Cornwall Morris Minor 1000 Club

Open to owners of Series M.M. cars and billed as the Club for Morris Minor owners West of the Tamar, this organisation has over 250 members. Benefits for members include regular meetings, a monthly newsletter and a second-hand spares service.
Club contact: Alan Jones, 10 Polstain Road, Threemilestone, Truro, Cornwall, England.

Morris Minor Registry/ Morris Owners Association of California

There are two main clubs in the U.S.A for Morris Minor Owners. Formed in the mid-1970s the Morris Registry and the Morris Owners Association of California operated for a time unaware of each other. They still remain independent organisations but they co-produce an interesting monthly magazine *Minor News.* Morris Minor Registry/Morris Owners Association of California, 2311 30th Avenue, San Francisco, CA94116, U.S.A.

Other Clubs

Amicale Morris Minor, Pierre Gravel, Rue du Moulin à vent, 37120 Richelieu, France.
Morris Minor Club Nederland, Halbe Tjepkema, Dijk 15, 2731 A.A., Benthuizen, Holland.
Nordisk Morris Minor Car Klubb, Box 8, 7300 Jelling, Denmark.
Morris Minor Registret of Sweden, Lennart Erickson, Laduvagen 1, S-781 34 Borlane, Sweden.

Morris Minor Car Club of New Zealand Inc., Julie Hunte, P.O. Box 12-245, Penrose, Auckland, New Zealand.

Morris Minor Car Club of South Africa, G.R. Dodds, 44 Fordyce Road, Walmer 6065, Port Elizabeth, South Africa.

Swiss Morris Minor Club, Patricia Bradley, Kleinzelglistr 12, 8952 Schlieren, Switzerland.

Morris Minor Group of British Columbia, c/o No. 1 1957 McNicoll Ave., Vancouver BC V6J 1A7, Canada.

Australian Clubs

Morris Minor Car Club of New South Wales, Maryann Kelly, P.O. Box 151, Earlwood 2206.

Geelong Morris Minor Car Club, Dennis Water, 26 & 28 Sparks Road, Norland 3214, & Graham Bullis, 347 Forest Street, Wendouree 3355.

Ballarat Morris Minor Club, Greg Andrews, P.O. Box 451, Ballarat 3350.

Central Victorian Morris Minor Car Club, Jan Stanford, P.O. Box 276, Bendigo 3550.

Twin City Morris Minor Car Club, Bob Wallis, 75 Chapple Street, Wodonga 3690.

Morris Minor Car Club A.C.T. & Southern, New South Wales, Micheal Bonfitto, 1/4 Chillagoe Street, Fisher 2611.

Wollongong Morris Minor Car Club, Linda Switzer, P.O. Box 64, Warrawong 2502 & Peter McGibbon, 41 Williamson Street, Corrimal 2518.

Hunter Region Morris Minor Car Club, Steve Ireland, 19 Alhambra Ave., Cardiff 2285.

Morris Minor Car Club of Queensland, Adrianne Myers, P.O. Box 419, Archerfield 4108.

Morris Car Club of Australia (Southern Australia), Inc., Don McNeill P.O. Box 37. Marden 5070.

Morris Car Club of Western Australia, Les Wilding, 25 Kadina Road, Gooseberry Hill 6076.

Morris Minor Car Club of Gold Coast, Rob Budford, 13 Lakeland Key, Miami Keys, Broadbeach 4217.

Morris Minor Car Club of Ipswich, Phil Holmes, c/o 42 Vineyard Street, Leichardt, Queensland 4305.

Morris Minor Car Club of Victoria, 12 Fairhills Parade, Glen Waverley 3150, Victoria.

Morris Register of Tasmania, The Registrar, Ken Watts, 130 Penquite Road, Launceston 7250, Tasmania.

Specialists

Morris Minor Centre, Avon House, Lower Bristol Road, Bath, England. Restoration work undertaken on the whole range of Morris Minors. Innovative scheme on 'Durable Car Ownership' launched in 1982.

Morris Minor Centre Spares Dept., Unit 5, Locksbrook, Avon Trading Estate, Bath, England. Sole B.L. Heritage parts supplier. Wide range of spares available but only a limited selection of specific M.M. lines in stock.

Morris Minor Centre Stormont, Hadden Road Industrial Estate, Woolwich, London SE28. London outlet for the Morris Minor Centre, Bath. A firm with some experience of early M.M. restoration.

Ask For Morris, Edinburgh Road, Cockenzie, East Lothian, EH32 0HY. Specialists in Morris Minor Sales, Service and Repairs. Comprehensive spares service including some M.M. parts.

South Yorkshire Morris Minors, Little Lane, Cusworth, Doncaster, South Yorks. Extensive range of spares including new and reconditioned parts. Full workshop facilities for restorations and conversions.

Morris Minor East Midlands, 71 Uppingham Road, Houghton on the Hill, Leicester, England. Suppliers of Morris Minor Centre spares. Special interest in earlier models. Restoration undertaken. Over the counter and mail order spares service.

John Black (Fenton) Ltd, Premier Garage, Victoria Road, Fenton, Stoke on Trent, ST4 2LJ. Morris Minor approved parts supplier. Specialist workshop for mechanical and bodywork repairs.

The Don Trimming Co. Ltd, Hampton Road, Erdington, Birmingham, B23 7JJ. England. Convertible hoods and side-screens supplied and fitted to individual requirements; also carpets, upholstery and trim.

Woolies (Ian and Caroline Woolstenholmes Ltd), off Blenheim Way, Northfields Industrial Estate, Market Deeping, Peterborough, PE6 8CD, England. This company specialises in items of trim.

Oldham and Crowther (Engineering) Ltd., 30 Ivatt Way, Westwood Industrial Estate, Peterborough, Cambridgeshire, PE3 7PG. Manufacturers of a complete underbody repair section and numerous body pressings. Membership of the Oldham and Crowther Restorers' Club is available and entitles members to preferential discounts on a wide range of products. International parts lists available.

Henric, Lortas Road, New Basford, Nottingham, England. Manufacturers and suppliers of replacement and repair panels. Morris Minor spares stockists. M.M. wing repairs undertaken, door repair panels available. M.M. 'tie plates' made.

Coventry Safety Glass Co., Bayton Road, Exhall, Coventry, England. Specialists in windscreens including making new split windows.

Derby Bearings Ltd., Siddals Road, Derby, DE1 2PZ, England. Ball and Roller Bearings Power Transmission Products. Stock complete range of bearings for M.M. cars.

P.D. Gough and Associates, 1 Bennerley Court, Blenheim Industrial Estate, Bulwell, Nottingham, NG6 8UT. England. Hand-made stainless steel exhausts made to order for M.M. cars. Discounts given to Owners' Club members.

M.W. Auto Electrics, Unit 2, North Street Industrial Estate, Brierley Hill, Birmingham, England. Auto electrcian specialists in Morris Minors 1948-71.

Overseas Specialists

Morriservice, 120 Fifth Avenue, Redwood City, California 94061. U.S.A. Largest stockist of Morris Minor parts in North America.

British Automotive Ltd, 579 Garfield Street, Eugene, Oregon 97402. U.S.A. Importers and suppliers of Morris parts including Morris Minor 1948-71.

Victoria British Ltd, Box 14991, Lenexa, Kansas 66215, U.S.A. Trim and accessories for all Morris Minors.

Morris Minor Centre of Australia, Bill Casburn (Proprietor), 246 Harbord Road, Brookvale, Sydney 2100, New South Wales.

The Morris Minor Company of Australia, Thorpe Renfrey (Proprietor), 19 Viking Court, Cheltenham, Victoria 3192, Australia.

Books

Apart from standard workshop manuals, owners' handbooks and the like, this is the first book to be published solely on Series M.M. Morris Minors. However, within many other Morris Minor publications reference is made to Series M.M. vehicles. The following list includes titles which the author feels may be of interest. Some (*) are publications contemporary with the cars' production years and are available only from Specialist Motoring bookshops or autojumble stall holders.

*The Morris Minor Series M.M. Workshop Manual.

The Morris Minor Series M.M. and Series II Workshop Manual. Both issued by Morris Motors Ltd. Available as Home and Export Editions.

*Morris Mono Construction, Morris Minor, Morris Oxford, Morris Six, 1950. Published by Morris Motors.
'A manual compiled to assist those concerned with the Rectification of Accident Damage to Morris Cars.' Contains a complete body parts list for Series M.M. cars including the four door saloon and exploded diagrams of construction along with useful ideas to assist with restoration.

*The Cassell Book of The Morris Minor by Ellison Hawks. Published by Cassell & Company Ltd. London 1958.
A miniature workshop manual for the Series M.M.

*The Book of The Morris Eight and The Morris Minor-Pitman's Motorist Library by Stanton Abbey. Published by Pitman and Sons Ltd., London.

*Morris Minor (including Series M.M., Series II and Minor 1000) Pearson's Illustrated Car Servicing for Owner Drivers, by D.V.W. Francis.
Hamlyn Publishing Group.

Morris Minor and 1000 Super Profile by Ray Newell. Haynes Publishing Group.
Companion to this volume tracing the development of subsequent models to the Series M.M.

Morris Minor: The World's Supreme Small Car by Paul Skilleter. Osprey.
Now in its 2nd edition. An award-winning publication which includes a useful section on the Series M.M.

Morris Minor 1948-70 by R.M. Clarke

Morris Minor Collection 1948-82. Brooklands Books. Collections of contemporary road tests, buying features and articles.

Practical Classics on Motoring Restoration
Published by P.P.G. Publishing Ltd. Although mostly concerned with the *Practical classics* restoration of a Minor 1000 Saloon this volume contains a wealth of information for the D.I.Y. restorer. Also contains a useful comparison of some of the Series M.M. cars featured in this book, with the V.W. Beetle.

Durable Car Ownership by Charles Ware.
Published by the Morris Minor Centre.
A book describing a revolutionary idea aimed at preserving the older car in general and the Morris Minor in particular.

PHOTO GALLERY

1. First prototype of the Mosquito dating from 1943, Code EX/SX/86, with narrower body than the eventual production model and significantly different front grille arrangement. (B.L. Heritage)

2. The interior of the 1943 Mosquito showing the column gear change for the 3-speed gearbox through which the 'flat-four' engine drove. Other significant features include the bench seat arrangement and the fascia. The louvres on the bonnet were an aid to the unique cooling system of the early prototypes which used a radiator located at the rear of the engine block. It was later moved to the more conventional forward position and the use of the louvres was discontinued. (B..L. Heritage)

3. No photographs exist of the original engines fitted to the Mosquito. This, similar, engine was fitted to the Morris Gutty, a small military vehicle being worked on by Morris and Issigonis. This is a 1949 model. (Roy Turner)

4. A 1948 pre-production car which resembles closely the Morris Minor Series M.M. Significant differences from earlier prototypes are the widened body with corresponding 4 inch strip in the bonnet, split bumper with concealed fillet, and an unusual badge arrangement. (B.L. Heritage)

5

HTX 836

6

7

HTX 836

8

OFC 771

9

10

5. Early production models were supplied with a rear light set-up like the one on this pre-production model: one reflector and one light. However, even the earliest production models were fitted with a boot badge complete with reflector – something this prototype didn't have. (B.L. Heritage)

6. Production models, like this one, had a split bumper blade and valance front and rear joined by a steel fillet. This was a legacy of the late decision to widen the car by 4 inches.

7. The Series M.M. Morris Minor was fitted with a 918cc side-valve engine. To many people it looked lost in the capacious engine bay.

8. Rear view of a very early production model. Circular rear lights are retained though they are not to original specifications. The boot badge with reflector was fitted as standard to this car.

9 & 10. The classic lines of the 'lowlight' Series M.M. ... showing the early type 'bulbous' front wings and the deep-cut rear wings ...

11. ... with new-style rear light fittings.

12. The rear lights were changed from a circular fitting to a helmet-type fitting with twin stop/tail lamps. This photograph also shows to good effect the flat bumper blade and the early-type rear valance mounting bracket.

13. The Morris Minor Series M.M. Tourer was manufactured with extra strengthening pieces to compensate for the loss of rigidity through having an open top.

14. Celluloid side screens were detachable and an 'envelope' was provided in which to store the hood when it was down.

15. The spare wheel carrier was not a standard production option! Once neatly tucked away in its envelope, the hood presented no problems. The detachable side screens were usually stored on top of the spare wheel in the boot of the car.

16. Contrasting piping was a feature of early interiors. Access to the rear seat was facilitated by hinged and folding front seats.

11

12

13

14

15

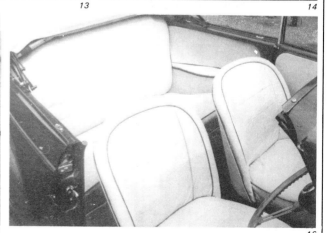

16

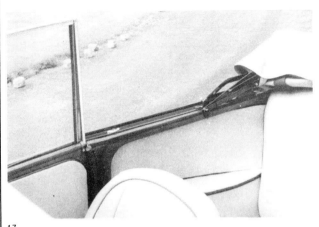

17

18

19

20

21

22

17 & 18.   The detachable side-screens were easily fitted and removed, though care had to be taken to fit them inside the hood when the top was up. Their main drawback was that they made the car draughty.

19.   Fitting a hood up is best done by two people. Care must be taken not to trap the material of the hood between the 'sticks' and all loose edges must be tucked in.

20.   For those with queries about the design of the first tourer hood, here is the answer. This early 1949 Tourer is destined for the American Market. Note the raised headlamps in the new-style wings and the 'pedestal type' rear lights. (B.L. Heritage)

21.   North American lighting regulations forced a change in the design of the Morris Minor series M.M. Here the new wing and front panel arrangement is being studied on the prototype American Minor in December 1948 – only a few months after production began. (B.L. Heritage)

22.   A 1950 M.M. Tourer L.H.D. export model. The original side lights have been changed to flashing indicators on this 'French' car. An indication of the restricted vision to the rear of the car is given in this picture. (Roy Turner)

23

24

25

26

27

28

23. L.H.D. fascia layout showing the plain central fascia grille and early-type motif on the glove locker. The arrangement of foot pedals is interesting particularly the position of the dip switch. (Roy Turner)

24. Early-type door pull arrangement with early-type ventilator catch assembly. (Roy Turner)

25. Later type Series M.M. door pull arrangement with later type ventilator catch assembly. (Roy Turner)

26. A 1951 2 door saloon fitted with a painted one-piece grille panel and plain painted hub caps. The change from chromium plated grilles and hub caps came about as a result of a temporary nickel shortage in 1951. On some 1951 models painted headlamp surrounds were fitted. (B.L. Heritage)

27. A 1951 M.M. Tourer. Rear view showing detachable side screens. The additional badge on the boot lid reads: Alta Overhead Conversion – a modification with which this vehicle is equipped. (Barbara Marshall)

28. A Series M.M. Tourer which exhibits all the original characteristics of the 1951 model. Early-type bonnet, painted grille, chrome hub caps and one-piece bumper. (Roy Turner)

29

30

31

32

33

29. The same car viewed with detachable sidescreens in place. (Roy Turner)

30. The same car viewed from the side with the hood up, showing the distinctive line of the bonnet and the new-style wings. (Roy Turner)

31. The distinctive badges from the Series M.M. placed conveniently on the flat strip of the bonnet ...

32. ... and on the boot lid – complete with reflector.

33. Early models were fitted with plain hub caps and had a distinctive circle painted on the wheel.

34.   Later models are fitted with hub caps embossed with 'M'. For a six month period in 1951 plain painted hub caps and painted hub caps with an 'M' were available. M.M. road wheels are not interchangeable with later Morris 1000 ones.

35.   Early Series M.M.s were fitted with small distinctive bonnet hinges – now very difficult to obtain – and had a different shaped bonnet from all subsequent Morris Minors.

36.   Later Series M.M.s had larger bonnet hinges. The bonnet also fitted differently as shown here.

37.   Early Series M.M.s can be distinguished by the absence of any moulding around the rear of the car.

38.   The moulding shown here was an additional styling feature on later models.

39.   When the Series M.M. 4 door saloon was introduced in October 1951 it was available for export only. Consequently early 4 doors are something of a rarity in Britain. This fine example is also something of a rarity in France where it was pictured in 1983. (Nicholas Pfeiffer)

40

41

42

43

44

45

40. This later picture of a L.H.D. model shows to good effect the interior seating arrangements and styling features of the 4 door saloon. Features worth noting include the ashtrays in the front door panel, the inclusion of a Smiths recirculatory-type heater and the changed position of the dip switch on the floor. (B.L. Heritage)

41. Over-riders were a later addition to the 4 door saloon.

42. Not all models were fitted with a heater as standard equipment. This 1952 Series M.M. saloon has no water pump fitted and the spaces provided for hoses to pass through the bulkhead are blanked off. Note the changed position of the coil from that of earlier models. (Roy Turner)

43. In contrast this 1952 model has a heater fitted. The hoses are clearly visible as is the water valve on the top of the engine block.

44. Fitting a heater required an additional modification to the bottom hose of the radiator – shown here.

45. 1952 Series M.M. 2 door saloon as seen from the front ...

46

47

48

49

50

51

46. ... and the side. This was how the Series M.M. looked after the ...

47. ... transitional period between low headlight and high headlight models ended. In the words of Reg Job, "changing the design of the wings was about all we got away with." Certainly the car was different in its overall appearance but it was still the same mechanically. Features to note – painted metal window-surround and 'M' motif hub caps.

48. A rear view of the interior of the 1952 Series M.M. 2 door saloon.

49, 50 & 51. Front, rear and side views of the 1952 Series M.M. Tourer. The most significant change in the later tourers was the introduction of fixed rear quarter lights. The advantage of this innovation was that it improved the general appearance of the car and made it more draught proof. Note the telltale line on the wing at the side of the headlamp denoting that later, '1000', wings have been fitted.

52

53

54

55

56

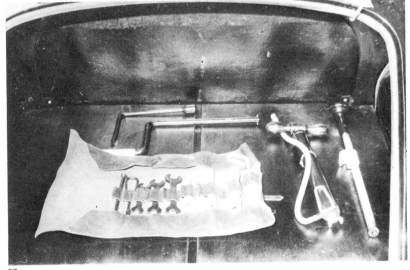

57

52.   The final layout of the Series M.M. fascia incorporating a central ashtray and an updated plastic glove locker badge.

53, 54 & 55.   Profile shots of the 1952 Series M.M. 4 door saloon. Features worth noting are the stainless steel window-surrounds, the contrasting painted grille, the owner-added rear reflectors and the plain rubber rear window-surround – the chromium insert had been discontinued in 1952.

56.   The publicity material made much of the luggage space of the new Morris Minor. The boot's capacity was 7 cu ft. In all Morris Minors the spare wheel was carried under the wooden floor of the boot.

57.   An adequate tool roll was supplied with each new car. Few will be as complete as this one.

58. A view of the rear seat in the 4 door saloon. If additional space was required for transporting bulky items the back rest of the seat, which was hinged, would fold forward to give access to the boot.

59. The first Morris Minor, NWL 576, as found in Sheffield in 1961 when it was exchanged for a Minor Million. It shows all the classic signs of rot and was clearly well used before it underwent complete restoration. (B.L. Heritage)

60. One of the major difficulties facing someone wishing to restore a 'lowlight' M.M. is finding a pair of replacement front wings. One solution is to have the 'rot' cut out, have part of a new wing manufactured and welded back in. The wing pictured has been repaired in this way.

61. Attention should always be paid to the structural strength of the car when it is being purchased. Serious rot at critical points such as the rear springs, shown here, will obviously indicate that major work will have to be done – not a job for the faint hearted!

62. A substantial part of the strength of a Morris Minor is in the central crossmember and in the inner sill boxing plates shown here. A careful examination of these areas should always be undertaken before any commitment to buy a vehicle is made. (Roy Turner)

63. The interior of the car should not be dismissed as unimportant either. Replacing leather faced upholstery like this can be expensive. (Roy Turner)

64

65

66

67

68

69

64.   This New Zealand-based Series M.M. is fitted with a Derrington Conversion. Courtesy of twin carburettors and a 'special' exhaust its acceleration and maximum speed are dramatically improved. (Colin Campbell)

65.   Another contemporary modification to increase the Series M.M.'s sluggish performance was the Alta Overhead Conversion. This popular conversion increased maximum speed to 76.5mph and retained good fuel economy. This engine is fitted to a home market Series M.M. Saloon which has been exported to the U.S.A. recently. (Guy Darisse)

66.   This contemporary photograph depicts an unusual highly personalised conversion fitted to a Series M.M. 2 door saloon in the mid '50s. (Daryll Clarke)

67.   It would certainly have been a contender for membership of the now defunct Modified Minor club whose badge is pictured here. (Barbara Marshall)

68.   Whether the tourer pictured on the left fitted with a Jarvis Hood Conversion would have qualified for entry is another matter. At £21, it was marketed as a coupé conversion for the Series M.M. tourer during 1949 by Jarvis and Sons Ltd of Wimbledon. A rear screen 'glass' could be fitted on request. (Autocar)

69.   The most successful venture into international rallying was the all-woman team of Betty Haig, Mrs 'Bill' Wisdom and Barbara Marshall, who finished 2nd in the Coupes Des Dames in the 1949 Monte Carlo Rally. (Autocar)

70

71

72

73

74

70.   Other less successful competitors entered and completed the course in later years. Henry Sutcliffe and his wife, who started the 1954 Monte in Athens and finished well down the field, are pictured here with their unusually 'well equipped' Series M.M. (National Motor Museum)

71.   Sedate rallying seemed more in keeping with the Series M.M.'s potential. This prized possession is seen going through its paces at Goodwood as part of the 1952 Brighton Rally. (National Motor Museum)

72.   A period picture of the Morris Minor Series M.M.'s successor, the Series II. Outwardly the only significant change was the bonnet badge and motif, but the presence of an O.H.V. engine under the bonnet heralded a new era in the development of the Morris Minor. (B.L. Heritage)

73.   Early brochure artwork featuring 2 door saloon ...

74.   ... and convertible models. Note the copy highlighting the 'big car' approach. (B.L. Heritage)

The NEW **MORRIS** MINOR

★ *The World's Supreme Small Car*

C1

Supreme in Comfort

Wider-than-ever seating, deep sprung for lasting ease—with all seats

within the wheelbase—and controlled ventilation give the **MORRIS MINOR** real "big-car" comfort

C2

C3

C4

C5

C6

C3 & 4. Early models were available in three colours: Romain Green, Platinum Grey and Black. The car pictured here has the unusually low Chassis Number SMM 507. At the time of writing it is the second oldest surviving Series M.M., the oldest being SMM 501, the first production model, which has been completely restored and 'resides' in Syon Park Museum. The car pictured here exhibits most of the original features and has undergone a full-scale restoration to a high standard. The tan interior with contrasting brown piping is completely original. Brown carpets were originally fitted too.

C5. The Morris Minor Series M.M. Tourer is a much sought-after vehicle and highly collectable. This particular vehicle is the one featured in the 'Owners' View' section of this book and it has undergone complete restoration.

C6. Detachable sidescreens give the Tourer a sporty look, though, with them removed, rear seat passengers emerge somewhat windswept after a long journey. Accessibility to the rear seat was made easy by 'tipping and folding' front seats.

C7

C8

C9

C7. The French Connection! A 1950 Series M.M. Tourer. This model exhibits the usual features associated with the 'transitional' vehicles. It retains many of the early M.M's features in spite of the new style wings and raised headlamps. This particular car was exported to Canada and then imported into France. It had only 27,000 miles recorded on the speedometer when photographed near Paris in 1983. (Roy Turner)

C8 & 9. A 1951 L.H.D. Series M.M. 4 door saloon. An unusual and very original car which exhibits some interesting features including the chromium insert in the rear windscreen rubber, which was fitted for a time to 4 door saloons. This particular car retains the chromium plated grille panel, plain hubcaps and the early-type bonnet with accompanying small hinges. Unlike later 4 door saloons it is not fitted with over-riders. (Roy Turner)

C10

C11

C10. A 1951 Series M.M. Tourer. Like its French counterpart featured earlier (C7) this home market Tourer retains many of the earlier features including the earlier type inner wings. It has however got a 'new' style grille which is painted body colour. Detachable sidescreens are retained and this particular model is fitted with a heater. (Roy Turner)

C11. With the hood down this is a striking car and one of the few remaining in Britain. This car has been restored and has served its lady owner well for sixteen years including two spent in Germany. (Roy Turner)

C12

C13

C14

C12. Black was a popular colour for Morris Minors and this particular car is exceptional. It is a 1952 Series M.M. 4 door saloon and it has been widely acclaimed, winning many Concours awards. Its owner is featured in the 'Owners' View'. Features noted earlier include the contrasting painted grille – common to black cars – and the over-riders which were fitted as standard on later 4 door series M.M. saloons.

C13. This picture shows to good effect the functional, uncluttered yet pleasant interior of the last of the M.M.s. The leather-faced 'bucket' type seats were surprisingly comfortable. The fascia changed little from the beginning of production except for the replacement of the metal glove locker badge by a plastic one, the introduction of an ashtray set in the fascia grille and the addition of letters on the control knobs.

C14. The engine compartment of the later M.M. This side-valve engine is complete with water pump and heater hoses. The side-valve engine may have looked lost in the large engine bay but one advantage of its physical size was the ease of access for maintenance.

Super Profile

C15

C16

C17

C15, A chance to compare and an opportunity to see the change in design which emerged during the production of the Series M.M. – a very different front end with a new bonnet design, new front wings, grille panel, bumper blades and valance not to mention bonnet hinges and hub caps.

C16. The 2 door M.M. was a very popular model. This particular car is very original and is in an unusual colour: Thames Blue. It has the painted grille typical of 1952 models and owner-added extras including a 'period' type internally adjustable radio aerial.

C17. This interior shot shows the contrasting upholstery with matching trim and the useful access to the rear seat gained by folding the passenger seat. Other features worthy of note are the metal glove locker badge, contrasting leather door pulls and the position of the semaphore indicators in the 2 door saloon.

C18

C19

C20

C18. The fixed rear quarter lights rather than detachable side screens had been introduced in 1951. This 1952 M.M. Tourer with its hood down shows them off to good effect.

C19. Morris Minor Series M.M. Tourers are hard to come by but even this one was 'lost' despite efforts to save it. (Bryan Gostling)

C20. Joining a recognised car club has untold benefits for owners of 'older cars'. The first Morris Minor produced, NWL 576, is seen here with hundreds of its successors at a Morris Minor Owners Club rally. Events like this are only one aspect of club activities. Most clubs endeavour to provide access to information, advice and even spares for their members. (Paul Davies)

Super Profile

C21

C22

C23

C21. NWL 576 at Cowley on the occasion of the Morris Minor Owners Club celebrations to mark the 35th anniversary of the beginning of Morris Minor production. Significantly this photograph is taken on the same spot where early prototypes like EX/SX/86 were photographed.

C22. Throughout production of the different Series the basic shape of the Morris Minor hardly changed. This is a Morris 1,000,000 of which 349 were produced, in 1961, to celebrate production's reaching that magic figure.

C23. A useful period, optional extra, which fitted into the glove locker lid, was a Smith's clock, pictured here.